THE SEARCH FOR
THE STONE OF DESTINY

THE SEARCH FOR
THE STONE OF DESTINY

Pat Gerber

Photographs by Andrew Morris

To Richard & Susan with best wishes for a lovely Holiday

Andrew Morris

July 2005

CANONGATE PRESS

First published in Great Britain in 1992 by
Canongate Press
14 Frederick Street
Edinburgh EH2 2HB

British Library Cataloguing-in-Publication Data
A catalogue record for this book is available
on request from The British Library

ISBN 0 86241 384 2

Printed and bound in Great Britain by
Butler & Tanner, Frome

PHOTOGRAPH ACKNOWLEDGMENTS

The publishers and author gratefully acknowledge permissions from the following sources:

Colour sections: HMSO; Historic Scotland

The Herald & Evening Times p 6, p 7, p 11, p 13, p 15, p 100, p 127 right and left, p 131;
The People's Palace, Glasgow p 18; Dr Graham Durant p 27; Hunterian Museum p 57;
Ronald Morris p 44, p 46; Mairi MacArthur p 52; Historic Scotland p 59, p 60

for Dad, Jane, Cyril, Penny and Bryony

Acknowledgements

Many people and institutions have helped in the making of this book. We are deeply grateful to all of them, in particular to: Professor Leslie and Elizabeth Alcock, Donald Anderson, Angus Rock Art, Arbroath Herald, Argyll Estates, Norman Atkinson, B.B.C. Radio Scotland, Professor G. Barrow, Catriona and Donald Bell, Jimmy Blain, British Library, British Museum, British Newspaper Library, Ian Brown, Buckingham Palace, Dr David Caldwell, Alastair Campbell of Airds, Ann and Peter Campbell, Danny Campbell, Bill Cameron, Bryony Carnie, Christopher Carnie, Jamie Carnie, Patrick Carnie, Penny Carnie, Clan Donald Centre, Catherine Crufts, Alastair J. Cuthbert, Clifford J. Denovan, Donald Dewar MP, Professor A.A.M. Duncan, Dundee Art Galleries and Museums, Dr Graham Durant, Neil Dougan, Bill Doig of the Herald and Evening Times Picture Library, Joan Earle, Eileen Eaton, Gillian Eatough, Edinburgh Castle, Professor A. Fenton, Marion C. Fentum, Finlaggan Trust, Ian Finlay, Cyril Gerber, Ian Hamilton QC, Margaret Harrison, Dr Hamish Henderson, Janette Henderson, P.H. Henderson, Herald, H.M.S.O., Dr Peter Hill, Sue Hillman, Historic Scotland, Jim Hume, the India Office Library, the Iona Community, Jordanhill College Library, Arnold Kemp, Dr Lawrence Keppie, Elspeth King, Gordon Leslie, Janice Lindsay, Dr E. Mairi MacArthur, Ian Macdonald QC, Sir Ian Bosville Macdonald of Sleate, Margaret Macdonald, Robert Macdonald, Sweyn and Lindsay Macdonald, Revd Uist Macdonald, Dr Norman MacDougall, Jimmie MacGregor, Sheila McGregor, Stuart McHardy, Lorn MacIntyre, Mhairi McIntyre, Ishbel McKenzie, Rona and Donald McKenzie, Archie McKerracher, Angus McKinnon, Dr Alasdair Maclean, B. Macleod, Bert McNulty, Professor John MacQueen, Lady Pamela Mansefield, Robyn Marsack, Elizabeth Marshall, Kay Matheson, Meigle Museum, A. Minty, Mitchell Library, Lady Naomi Mitchison, Professor Rosalind Mitchison, Alistair Moffat, Montrose Museum, Ronald W. B. Morris, the National Library of Scotland, Revd John Mackay Nimmo, the National Museums of Scotland, Norman Newton, Sir Iain Noble, the People's Palace, Christine Primrose, Erina Rayner, Christine Reynolds, Florence Russell, School of Scottish Studies, Scone Palace, Scotsman, Scottish Record Office, Scottish Television, George Shepherd, Jim Sillars MP, Jamie Sinclair, George Smith, John Smith MP, Somerset House, Harry Stanger Ltd, Emma St John-Smith, David Stewart, Alan Stuart, Ronald Stuart, Nigel Tranter, Lisbeth M Thoms, University of Glasgow, University of Edinburgh, University of St Andrews, Margaret Walker, Whithorn Trust, Rob Welsh, Westminster Abbey, Margaret Wilson, Brian Wilton, Daphne and George Wyllie, Sue Youngs.

We are grateful to the following for permission to use illustrations: The Herald, H.M.S.O., Historic Scotland, The People's Palace, The Hunterian Museum, Dr Graham Durant, Ronald Morris and Mairi MacArthur. Every effort has been made to trace owners of copyright and we apologise to any whom it has proved impossible to contact.

Contents

INTRODUCTION *xi*

Part I
CARRIED AWAY AT CHRISTMAS *1*
THE HOSTAGE STONE *9*
QUEENS, KINGS AND CORONATION CHAIRS *16*

Part II
HOW THE LEGENDS BEGAN *19*
JACOB AND THE THUNDER STONES *26*
IRELAND *31*
ROMANS AND CHRISTIANS *35*
DALRIADA AND THE ROYAL BOAR *43*
COLUMBA KING OF STORMS *48*
DUNSTAFFNAGE *57*

Part III
SCOTLAND UNITED? *61*
WHO OWNS SCOTLAND? *66*
ENGLAND'S EDWARD AND THE CELTIC FRINGES *71*
WALLACE AND THE MISSING STONE *77*
ROBERT THE BRUCE *80*

Part IV
LORD OF THE ISLES *87*
THE SEARCH FOR THE STONE OF SKYE *93*
THE KNIGHTS TEMPLAR *97*

Part V
SIR WALTER SCOTT AND EDINBURGH CASTLE *101*
MACBETH'S CASTLE *105*
A ROYAL PECULIAR *112*
THE STONE OF DESTINY *118*
FREEDOM COME-ALL-YE *124*

REFERENCE SOURCES AND BIBLIOGRAPHY *133*

THE WEE MAGIC STANE

O the Dean o' Westminster wis a powerful man
He held a' the strings o' the State in his hand
And a' this great power it flustered him nane
Til some rogues ran away wi' his wee magic stane.

Wi a tooreli ooreli ooreli ay etc

Noo the stane had great powers that could dae such a thing
For withoot it it seemed we'd be wantin' a king.
So he called in the polis and gave this decree
Go and hunt oot the stane and return it tae me.

So the polis went keekling way up tae the north
They hunted the Clyde and they hunted the Forth,
But the wild folk up yonder just pitied them a'
For they didnae believe it wis magic at a'.

Noo the Provost o' Glesga Sir Victor by name
He was very pit oot when he heard o' the stane,
So he offered the statues that stand in George Square
That the High Churches might mak a few mair.

When the Dean of Westminster with this wis acquent
He sent for Sir Victor and made him a saint.
'But it's no use you sending your statues down heah'
Said the Dean, 'but you've given me a jolly good idea'.

So he quarried a stane o' the very same stuff
And he dressed it all up till it looked like enough,
Then he sent for the press and announced that the stane
Had been found and returned tae Westminster again.

When the thieves found out what Westminster had done
They ran aboot diggin' up stanes by the ton
And for each one they finished they entered the claim
That this wis the real and original Stane.

But the cream o' the joke still remains tae be tellt
Fur the bloke that wis turnin' them aff on the belt
At the peak o' production wis sae sorely pressed
That the real yin got bunged in alang wi' the rest.

So if ever ye come on a Stane wi' a ring
Just sit yersel' doon and proclaim yersel' King.
For there's nane wid be able tae challenge yer claim
That ye'd crowned yersel' King on the Destiny Stane.

Johnny McEvoy

Introduction

Where is the Stone of Destiny? While historians protest that England's Edward 1 reived it from Scotland back in 1296, archaeologists and ordinary folk hunt for it up mountains, in castles, beneath lochs and bogs, for Stone stories are part of Scottish folklore. The reappearance of the Coronation Stone north of the border in 1951 generated strong feelings, not only in Scotland, but around the globe.

Edward 1 plundered the Stone to weaken Scottish morale. Seven hundred years later his actions still haunt the relationship between Scotland and England, in spite of all manner of treaties of union, and that relationship affects every single person living and working in Scotland today.

The context in which we live matters to us. The shared experience of growing up and working in Glasgow, Scotland is quite different from that of growing up and working in Ireland, Israel or India: the folkore helps form our collective national personality. We all declare membership of several groups, one of the most important being the culture from which we come. Folk traditions are taught in schools precisely to help children identify, not only with the cultures from which they come, but also with that in which they are growing up. At the very least we have a curiosity about our parents, an emotional bond whether it be hate or love or something in between for the place in which we grew up, and a feeling of community with the race or races from which we originate—their folklore and their idiosyncracies.

Is there a precedent, anywhere in the world, for a stone being venerated in quite the same way as the Stone of Destiny, and for such a long time? Who is the actual owner of that bugged rock that lies beneath the Coronation Chair? And why are we, people of late 20th-century Europe—sophisticated, materialistic as never before—still so fascinated by magic? The Stone of Destiny has intrigued story-tellers from Miss Jane Porter and her Victorian contemporary Sir Walter Scott to twentieth century novelists like Compton McKenzie and Nigel Tranter. Recently it has turned up in science-fiction thanks to American rock music critic Patricia Kennealy, who links the story with Arthurian legend.

In recent times legends have been kept for children, along with fairy tales but, in view of the mass destruction of documentary evidence in Scotland caused by fire, pillage, mildew and ecclesiastical Reform, and a growing realisation of the value of our folk heritage, our historians have evolved new routes into the past, one of which is through folklore. The legend of the Stone of Destiny links into other Scottish traditions—the Loch Ness Monster, even the doings of Lancelot and Guenevere—and their stories shadow the movement of people and ideas through the Dark Ages till they arrive in the perceived daylight of the present century.

English antiquarian Thomas Pennant (1726-98) was one of Scotland's earliest tourists. He

How one Scot feels about Scotland—George Wyllie and his Destiny Stones.

provides the first full written story about the Stone of Destiny. He is at Scone:

In the church of the abbey was preserved the famous chair, whose bottom was the fatal stone, the palladium of the Scottish monarchy; the stone, which had first served Jacob for his pillow, was afterwards transported into Spain, where it was used as a seat of justice by Gethalus, contemporary with Moses. It afterwards found its way to Dunstaffnage in Argyll, continued there as the Coronation Chair till the reign of Kenneth 11, who, to secure his empire, removed it to Scone. There it remained, and in it every Scottish monarch was inaugurated till the year 1296, when Edward I, to the mortification of North Britain, translated it to Westminster Abbey, and with it, according to ancient prophecy, the empire of Scotland.

To whom does the Stone matter today? The answer lies in the actions of those who believe they have it in their keeping. So important is it to the monarchy, to the established Church of England, and to the people of Britain, that they corral it in the most effective security system human ingenuity can devise. They won't discuss it—in case its essence escapes to stir up controversy? Clearly they would quite like the physical entity of the Coronation Stone to stay put, regardless of treaties and questions about its ownership. Possession is all.

Several stones are also kept under conditions of tight security in Scotland. The hiding-place of a Hebridean Stone is handed down only from father to son—we are not told what happens if the heir is a daughter. Anonymous letter-writers tell of Stones scattered over the landscapes of Scotland like raisins in a scone. There are mystics, ministers, lords and lay-people who know of the whereabouts of other stones, and who will tell, when the time is ripe. Self-styled sculptor [sic] George Wyllie was recently seen mixing carry-out Destiny Stones.

The legends to which we are the heirs overlap and contradict each other. They are riddled with tantalising gaps over which writers have taken colossal imaginative leaps—which is how new stories begin.

Nevertheless, we shall set out bravely to attempt a closer look. What sources can we tap? Where is the thin fabric of fact patched with wishful thinking?

The main thread of the story, as related by Pennant, comes from some of the earliest known writings of homo sapiens, and perhaps even from the exploding of some comet in outer space. It winds along the routes of tribal movement from Israel to Egypt, Greece, Spain, up the western coast of France to Brittany, Ireland and thence to Scotland. All the tales come together at Scone in the tenth century, then fray out into yet more, ranging from Islay, Iona and Skye, across the breadth of Perthshire, to Edinburgh Castle, from Whithorn and Melrose in the borders to the shores of the Moray Firth.

Was Scota an ancestor of the present Queen? What made Scota want to voyage to the damp and chilly north? Why did Nennius bother to write her story? Why did Columba follow Jacob's fad for sleeping on stone pillows? Exactly what is it that makes a royal personage need to lower her posterior onto an old Stone from Scotland, in public, before she can truly feel queen of the United Kingdom?

Some questions may prove unanswerable, given the present state of knowledge and the limitations of the writer, but it is hoped that the reader, whether erudite or merely curious, will find this book interesting, and perhaps even useful as a starting-point for further researches, and that a platform will have been built for discussion and debate.

Several people in Scotland are currently taking an interest in the whereabouts of the Stone, and have kindly offered the fruits of their research.

The information collected comes from the work of story-tellers, archaeologists, song-writers, historians, farmers, churchmen, sculptors, genealogists, journalists, kings, advocates, seers, accountants, knights, academics, dreamers, aristocrats, teachers, travellers, politicians and poets. Letters and phone-calls have come not only from Scottish addresses, but also from England, Canada, the United States, Africa, Australia and New Zealand. Clearly there must be some truth in the belief that, although there may be 5,000,000 people in Scotland, the world as a whole is the richer by an estimated 90,000,000 emigré-Scots.

Folk tales have a kinetic energy of their own. In writing them down, one risks making them

Mairi MacArthur whose great-grandfather found 'St Columba's Pillow'

too definite, incapable of re-interpretation. Duncan Williamson, the Traveller-story-teller, reluctantly permits his stories to be published, feeling that the process of writing can kill a story dead, so that it becomes nothing more than a specimen for scientific inspection, like a pinned butterfly. A real tale should be free to move, according to the mood of the day, the audience, the time of year. Each nation once had its own oral tradition, its folklore handed down, like the old game of Whispers, to grow and fade, mutate, and live again in every telling.

Yet perhaps, in an age when everything we value has to come with documentation, to collect what is known, what has been discovered, what is being researched, what traditions there are about the Stone, is permissible so that future folklorists may have a central starting point. Maybe to read the lore is to understand a little better why the people of Scotland are as they are. In order that you, the reader, are as free as possible to make up your own mind about the Stone, or indeed Stones, based on your own particular thoughts, your knowledge, your interests, biases and perceptions, some of the evidence is presented in its raw state for your consideration. While there has necessarily been selection, and some things have had to be omitted for lack of space, as much as possible is included for the reader to interpret and to use.

Donald and Catriona Bell, members of the Finlaggan Trust, Islay, involved with excavation of a new site: the stronghold of the Lords of the Isles.

The Dochart Falls

PART I

1. Carried Away at Christmas

Probably the best known story about the Stone is that of the group of students who spirited it out of Westminster Abbey in December 1950 and took it to Scotland. The adventures of that winter have been brilliantly recounted in the autobiographies of one of the protagonists, Ian Hamilton, but in order to see it in its historical context we should perhaps begin with a glance at that event.

For a long time it was believed that Edward 1 had indeed got away with the ancient Stone of Destiny in 1296 and, as Scotland developed after the Union and began to find a renewal of interest in itself thanks partly to the novels of Sir Walter Scott, the imprisonment of the Stone became, for some, a symbol of England's treatment of the people of Scotland.

In the late nineteenth century this feeling began to give rise to a series of plots to bring the Stone back. The first of these proved unsuccessful, but the attempts appealed to the Scots' sense of humour and received wide press coverage, encouraging discussion of Home Rule and keeping the topic on the boil. In 1886 a Counsellor at Law, Eric Macdonald Lockhart, published a pamphlet in which he wrote: 'There has been a growing up of *Centralisation* in Westminster, and a movement in the opposite direction is now very much required'. He went on: 'If the truth must be told, Scotland has never occupied her own proper place in the councils of the Nation,

since the Union was scandalously carried through in 1707'. He advocated federal union between the nations of Britain, and self-government for Scotland.

By early in the twentieth century, between fighting two terrible wars, Scottish writers, lawyers and leading thinkers continued the debate. They looked for ways to stir up the Scottish people sufficiently to effect the political changes they wanted. It was very hard to do. The attitude of Scots seemed to be that politicians and those with power too frequently misuse it, while the ordinary person is powerless—although permitted to vote, you couldn't change anything—so shrug the shoulders, keep the head down and get on with real life. Alright—if you couldn't catch the public's imagination by haranguing at street corners, give them a laugh. And while they were laughing they might open their ears and minds for long enough to believe that change was possible.

Several factors came together to fix the idea of bringing the Stone back to Scotland in the minds of some individuals. Compton Mackenzie's *The North Wind Of Love* (1944) included his plot to rescue the Stone on St Andrew's Day 1932. Nigel Tranter's *The Stone* (1958) has a research team from Oxford University digging up the stone Edward I failed to find, thus forcing questions about it into the open. Clearly the captive Stone

1

was seen by these people, too, as a symbol of the Scottish people, who they saw also as being sat upon by the dominant English. The poet Hugh MacDiarmid supported the cause, and the actor Duncan MacRae was involved in an actual attempt to take the Stone. At that time the first replica stone was cut, intended as a replacement while the conspirators got away with the real one. A monumental sculptor in Glasgow, Robert (Bertie) Gray kept it in his yard for many years, and more copies may have been made later.

above Ian Hamilton QC
opposite Plan of Westminster Abbey

Scottish service personnel coming home from war in the late forties, having seen their friends killed and maimed in the name of democracy, believed Scotland had come of age, had won the right to demand reform. Some disseminated their ideas at universities, and even those of us still at school picked up the excitement and went fly-posting and slogan-painting at night.

But the Labour government proved uninterested in the failing economies of the north, and the tiny Scottish National Party hadn't yet caught on. Then, in November 1949, a Glasgow lawyer, Dr John MacCormick, launched the Scottish Covenant, which had more moderated ideals than the SNP. Members sought reform and self-government, but remained loyal to the Crown. On a tidal wave of optimism MacCormick was elected Rector of Glasgow University, and by June 1950 a seventh of the Scottish electorate had joined. Students thirled themselves to the cause, including Kay Matheson, Ian Hamilton, Gavin Vernon and Alan Stuart.

That year the Conservative Party under Churchill was returned to power and Scotland was virtually disenfranchised. Ian Hamilton, studying law at Glasgow University, decided something had to be done and, when he met Kay at a Covenant party that October, found her in a similar frame of mind.

Kay, a trainee teacher, was born in Inverasdale, Rosshire, 'the year the Scottish National Party was formed', December 1928. She is a small, gently-spoken woman with a wry sense of humour, who looks directly at you and takes time to think before she speaks, preferring Gaelic to English. 'I'm still hoping that we will get self-government.'

She thought Hamilton arrogant, but liked his enthusiasm and commitment.

Hamilton remembers her ethereal quality— she was 'remote as a Hebridean island'. Three years her senior, slightly built himself, highly intelligent and a bit of a loner, he had been a nationalist since his schooldays. He believed parliament must pay heed to the serious requests coming from Scotland. Otherwise frustration would erupt into to violence. Militancy was in the air. Westminster greeted the Scottish Covenant with the collective yawn it reserved for the lunacies of the Celtic fringe. The Scots, irritating as their own midges, were moaning again. Politicians had more important things to attend to.

Hamilton thought if only he could succeed in bringing the Stone back to Scotland it would be a symbolic, political and bloodless gesture. He also thought the outcome for himself would certainly be jail and the wreckage of his legal career. It did not occur to him that people might write off the escapade as a student prank.

In September 1950 he reconnoitered Westminster Abbey. Back in Glasgow he researched in the Mitchell library. He decided to make his attempt in the Christmas break. He needed a car, money, burglar's tools and confederates. Who could he trust? Financial backing to the tune of £10 came from a Glasgow businessman who had been involved in the thirties attempt. Bertie Gray was a monumental sculptor as well as a Glasgow councillor and vice-chairman of the Covenant, produced his replica of the Stone from his Lambhill store.

At the end of every Michaelmas Term, Glasgow University holds an all-night ball known as Daft Friday. Kay Matheson accompanied Ian Hamilton.

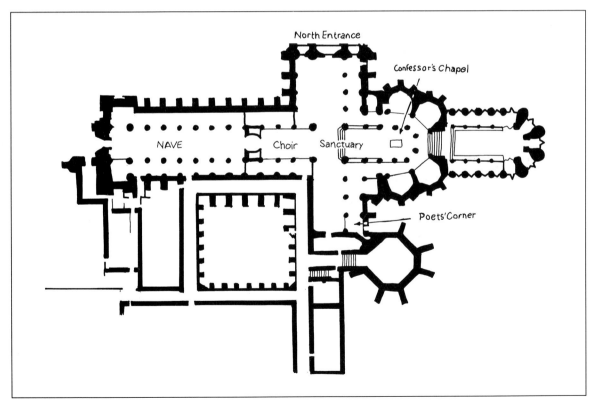

She was discreet. Nobody would suspect such a pretty girl, the innocence shining out of her. He told her his plans. Kay thought he was pulling her leg. She listed those who had failed— Wendy Wood, Hugh MacDiarmid, John MacCormick himself. What made Ian think he'd succeed? He told her.

'And what am I to do?' she had asked. 'I suppose I was the obvious choice. I wasn't a nervous sort of person—and I could drive. They thought a lassie would not be suspected, and that I might be likely to bring the Stone back to Scotland more safely than a man would.'

They recruited Gavin Vernon, an easy-going student, and planned their journey. But on the afternoon of Friday 22nd December, when they went to collect him, another student, Alan Stuart, was there, desperate to help, and offering another car. It was safer to take him than to leave him in Glasgow to talk. Soon they were speeding south through the frosty night.

So many things went wrong. On his first attempt on the evening of Saturday 23rd, Hamilton was ejected by the night watchman. Feeling 'pretty sick' at letting the others down, he caught up with them around the Christmas tree in Trafalgar Square.

Kay refused to go home without the Stone. They would sleep in the cars. They did—and nearly froze. She caught flu. Defeat stared them in the face. Hamilton tried to persuade her to go home. Instead, she checked in at an hotel for a few hours sleep. London was celebrating Christmas Eve. The police were usefully occupied with singing, fighting drunks and, by 2 a.m. on Christmas morning, the streets had quietened. Hamilton, Vernon and Stuart reconnoitered the outside of the Abbey. They went to collect Kay, but the hotel manager was suspicious. So was Kay, who heard him phoning. She arrived downstairs to see a detective questioning Hamilton about the car, which he thought was stolen. They

got rid of him—but not before he had taken its registration number.

Once again Hamilton began to doubt whether they should proceed—and once again Kay's resolution kept them going. Big Ben struck 4 a.m. as Kay drove the Anglia into a lane at Palace Yard by the Abbey. Hamilton had parked the known car on nearby Millbank. She stayed in the car as the others broke in to the Abbey near Poets' Corner and made for the Confessor's Chapel. Hamilton laid his coat reverently on the ground to receive the Stone, but it wouldn't budge. He pulled one of the rings, and suddenly it was sliding towards him as easily as though the hands of angels were helping. To his horror he realised that only part of the sandstone block was attached to the ring.

Heaving it like a rugby ball, he sprinted out to dump it in the car. Dashing back in to the Abbey, he helped manoevre the main part onto his coat. They started to slide it out through the door. Suddenly Kay started the car. Hamilton left the others, ran down the lane and leapt into the passenger seat. What was she thinking about? They weren't ready to leave yet.

She whispered 'A policeman is coming towards us' and promptly melted into Hamilton's arms. So affected was the constable by the young lovers that he spent time kindly explaining where they could find a darker car-park. He also divulged that no bobby would be keen to make an arrest that night, for he wouldn't want to spend Boxing day in court. But when he left they knew the Anglia's number was also now on record. Kay decided to get her part of the Stone out of London immediately. 'We didn't break it, you know. It had been cracked by a suffragette's bomb.'

A traffic light stopped her outside Harrods in Knightsbridge. When she started off again there was a loud thump. She pulled in. 'Ian hadn't closed the boot properly, and the Stone had landed in the middle of the road. I had to lift it back in again—but I had the muscle, from carrying the peats. I probably had more muscle than Ian did at that time.'

She drove to a friend's house in Birmingham. Mary Chalk shared digs with Kay in Glasgow, and although somewhat surprised to see her, gave her a welcome, a garage for the Anglia, and a credulous ear for the story Kay had created. They were expecting a guest for Christmas lunch.

He turned out to be the Chief Constable of Birmingham. 'It wasn't funny at the time', says Kay. 'When he came in I thought they had discovered everything.' But she kept her nerve, fighting off fatigue and the encroaching weakness of flu, keeping his mind off his work by playing party games with him. When the lunchtime news came over the radio about the disappearance of the Stone, 'The paper hat nearly flew off my head. But he never suspected a thing'.

'Well then the news was out,' Kay went on. 'The border roads were closed—for the first time in four hundred years. So I went and stayed with another friend in Scarborough. She was delighted to keep me until the borders were opened again.'

As soon as it was safe to travel she made her way north to her mother in Inverasdale, after her Christmas 'holiday'. The Anglia and its cargo were still in the garage in Birmingham.

Meanwhile, Hamilton had collected the spare car from Millbank. The other two members of his team, Vernon and Stuart, had vanished. End-over-end, he heaved the Stone onto the back seat. 'I think it went quite easily . . . the hands of God were over mine'. Filled with wild elation, he drove south—the police would block all roads north. A good idea—but how do you know which way is south in an unfamiliar town in the dark? When dawn came he was still being misdirected around London by strangers. In-

credibly, he spotted Vernon and Stuart.

Vernon was despatched to wait while Hamilton and Stuart sped towards Kent and planked the Stone on a grassy bank. They returned to Westminster, where Hamilton retrieved his coat, and worried about what his father, a Paisley tailor, would say about the dreadful state he had got it into. That night they drove down the frosty roads of Kent, collected the Stone, and went hunting for a better hiding place. At the edge of a wood by an airfield near Rochester, they hollowed out a hiding-place in some scrubby grass. The Stone should be safe there.

Expecting arrest at any moment, they posted a rough map of the Stone's hiding place to friends in Glasgow, and headed north.

They were stopped by police near Doncaster. Had they seen the Coronation Stone? Hamilton said firmly that it should have been taken back to Scotland years ago. Stifling a yawn, the policeman waved them on. That night, very late and very exhausted, they arrived at the Stuart's Barrhead home to a warm welcome and a whisky apiece.

Stuart's father was a builder. He told them the Stone, after six dry centuries in the Abbey, might now be soaking up dampness by day, and splitting into crumbs in the nightly frosts. Vernon cheerfully envisaged shovelling it into paper pokes to bring it home. Bertie Gray reassured them. But Hamilton, who genuinely revered the Stone, blamed himself for putting it at risk. Kay had invited Stuart to spend New Year at Inverasdale, but instead he found himself driving south again with Hamilton.

The worst thing for Hamilton was not knowing how much the police knew—surely they must have some information? Were the police watching any of them? Would it be possible to retrieve the Stone before Scotland Yard caught up with them?

Late in December, leaving Bertie Gray to

above Kay Matheson; *opposite (from left)* Councillor Bertie Gray,
Gavin Vemon, Ian Hamilton and Alan Stuart, 1951

deliver an anonymous petition to the press, Hamilton and Stuart set off south in the Stuart family's large Armstrong-Siddeley, down frozen roads on packed snow with the AA warning of blizzards to come. There were two new members of the team: the late Johnny Josselyn, 'a strange, wild, brilliant character,' an Englishman who worked for the admiralty in Bath, but who had been educated in Scotland and was a strong Scotophile, and Bill Craig, the President of Glasgow University Union who had been unable to go with them on the first journey. The weather slowed them considerably and they didn't reach London till the following night. At a cafe they read a headline in the *Star,* STONE: ARRESTS EXPECTED SOON. Were they driving straight into an ambush? They had few choices. To go home without the Stone and risk its disintegration? Or to go on towards Rochester and risk capture?

In Kent they began to recognise landmarks. But when they reached the place where they thought they'd hidden the Stone, they saw only the flickering flames of a gypsies' bonfire. They drove on. They came back. The gypsies were encamped exactly on the spot where the Stone lay.

It was too much of a coincidence. The 'gypsies' could only be detectives in fancy dress, waiting to pounce. But the thought of all these policemen in their gypsy gear cheered the young men up. What had they to lose by taking a

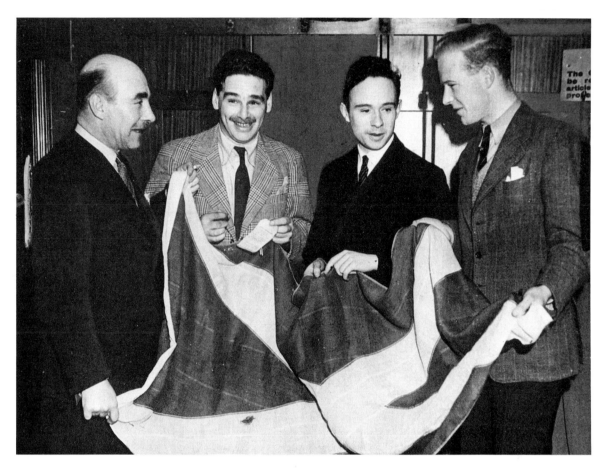

chance? To go back to Scotland with empty hands would be intolerable. Later Hamilton wrote of the gypsies: 'Out of all the broad acres of England, why should they have chosen that spot on that night?' For nothing could have hidden the Stone from the police better.

He descibes how he and Craig walked slowly down across the field. 'In the leaping flames we could see an ancient gypsy couple sprawled against the fence, their boots outstretched to the blaze. The man could have put his hand through the fence and touched the Stone.' Craig asked if they could have a heat at the fire. Welcomed in, he sat for a long time without saying anything.

Hamilton had often had cause to admire Craig'spersuasive tongue, his ability in debate, and clearly that night he had cause to admire his reticence too. Eventually Craig began to talk of the cold, and gently, with many pauses, steered the conversation to the situation of Travellers, how they were constantly harried, about the need for rights and freedom, and of the Scottish people in the north who, like the gypsies, were trying to retain their ways and their freedoms and how, in order to achieve certain aims in that direction, he urgently needed something that was behind the caravan.

Two of the gypsies courteously helped carry

the Stone to the car, where it was placed in lieu of the passenger seat and covered with a travelling rug. Hamilton still feels 'despicable' when he remembers how he mistakenly offered money in thanks. It was politely refused. The whole incident has for him an element almost of the supernatural: 'Sometimes I wonder if they werereally there, yet they must have been, for we all saw and spoke to them. But why? Out of all the broad acres and highways and lanes of England, why on that exact spot? Within one yard? Why on that exact night of all nights?'

Taking turns at sitting on the Stone, they drove north up the A6. At York Johnny was reluctantly dropped at the station with the real passenger seat, to continue his journey by train. A Yorkshire petrol pump operator said cheerily that the police had been there earlier asking what Scotsmen he'd sold petrol to. Hamilton managed to hold his nerve long enough to make a crack about the Stone being in the boot. Exhaustion and nervous tension, as the border approached, were beginning to affect him.

At half past two that Hogmanay they drove the Stone of Scone across the border and into Scotland. Hamilton writes: Success is a strange thing, much nearer to tears than to laughter.' A few miles further on they stopped, to expose the Stone to Scottish air 'for the first time in six hundred years', and to pour a libation of whisky over it, and to drink a toast—to the Stone, to each other, and to the new Scotland they were going to build.

Later that evening they drove into Glasgow. The whole adventure had cost a total of £70. And they had no idea whatsoever what to do with their cargo. Hamilton phoned Bertie Gray, and while they waited for him outside the King's Theatre in Glasgow, he found himself munching a fish supper, sitting on the Stone in the car. 'I had never been in a more bizarre situation.'

When Gray arrived he said: 'Drive out towards Stirling. I've got the very man.' All those involved now faced arrest, prosecution and imprisonment. Others were destined to whisk the Stone into hiding. And so the Stone of Scone was back in Scotland. Did anybody know? Did anybody care? And did Hamilton and his confederates succeed in their aim of arousing the Scottish people in any way?

2. The Hostage Stone

The people of Scotland knew the Stone had gone missing, but they had no idea where it was, or who had taken it. Had our ancient and most highly venerated relic been hidden safely by responsible, if misguided, idealists? Were a bunch of silly students taking risks with it for the sake of a prank? Were some cranks about to dispose of it? Concern was expressed in the newspapers and on radio, and King George himself was anxious about its safety. Clearly he believed the Stone affair could have far-reaching consequences.

The late John Rollo was lunching in his works canteen on Christmas Day 1950, listening to the one-o'clock news on radio. Till then he had known nothing of the plot to take the Stone, and when he heard what had happened he was very amused. A benevolently-inclined industrialist who worked on the executive committee of the National Covenant, Rollo was blissfully unaware of the part he was about to play. Singer and broadcaster Jimmie MacGregor remembers 'the ripple of delight that ran through Scotland when we heard that The Stone had returned. It was a great joke, and we admired the sheer nose-thumbing cheek of the venture. We were aware that another buttress had been erected against the crumbling fabric of our identity'. He and partner Robin Hall began to sing Johnny McEvoy's composition *The Wee Magic Stane*.

Because nobody had any idea where the Stone was, or what sort of people had taken it, rumours were whizzing about. Worldwide, newspapers were publishing articles and letters—with varying degrees of accuracy. Journalists were breaking legs in the race for 'scoops'.

Stone Still Missing— wrist-watch found— people who took it are cranks— Block of concrete dredged up from Serpentine— Petition to the King left at a Glasgow newspaper office— Scottish Dean of Westminster, Dr A. C. Don has left London for 3 days rest. The Dean had not gone to Scotland— police inquire into recent activities of student . . .

Two days after the disappearance of the Stone Dr A. C. Don, the Scottish Dean of Westminster, addressed the nation. He spoke of his feelings when the Clerk of Works had rushed into his bedroom and told him that the Coronation Stone had gone. Never, till this week had anyone dared to lay sacreligious hands on this precious relic which was treasured by millions and the King had let him know that he was greatly distressed. Listeners were told to keep their eyes and ears open— and that Don would 'go to the ends of the earth to fetch it back'. His agitation was understandable. King George knew privately that he had only a few months to live, and wanted to be sure that his daughter would be properly crowned, on the Stone. People had a

9

real affection for the King, quite different from the mixture of speculation, adulation and ridicule showered on royalty today. Public apologies began to pour southward. The SNP, attempting to gain respectability, wrote to him deploring the way 'ill-disposed persons' were embroiling him in a controversy about national property 'unlawfully acquired' and saying that the 'theft' had revived racialist tendencies.

While Glasgow University creaked its ancient bones into celebrating five centuries of existence, legal and political questions were aired—the Stone belonged neither to King nor Church but to the Scottish people. If the Scots people had proper constitutional means of expressing their will . . . was this felony or larceny, or hooliganism? The American journal *Time* devoted a whole page to the Stone.

Scots began to worry about what the neighbours thought. The act was perpetuating superstition, bringing ridicule on Scotland's 'Stone Age' mentality. John Cameron KC, a prominent Covenant leader, and Dr Neville Davidson, Minister of Glasgow Cathedral, pleaded for the return of the Stone to Westminster. Scots should seek legal means to have its custody in Scotland, if their reform requirements were to be taken seriously.

Meanwhile, Scotland Yard was still busy hunting for clues. After the wrist-watch, someone found a plaque about the Stone on a bombsite 500 yards from the Abbey. Some blamed the English. England's refusal to restore the Stone to Scotland themselves, as a civilised neighbour, had resulted in the loss of this Scottish national relic.

But a meeting was held in St Andrew's Hall, Glasgow, at which the perpetrators of 'the glorious deed' were cheered. Dr Mary Ramsay challenged the audience 'If the men of Scotland cannot find a way to get it (the Stone), then the women of Scotland certainly will', to applause.

Scotland Yard discovered that Cromwell's bust had been knocked sideways. Eventually they were driven to employ a Dutch medium. Sensible folk earned a bob or two selling plaster models of the Coronation chair and Stone to London's tourists. The late Wendy Wood, a lifelong Scottish Nationalist, wrote energetically about how the retrieving of the Stone of Destiny had produced national panic in England, and a rejuvenation of national consciousness in Scotland. England, she said, 'wailed like a war siren . . . forgetting . . . that one of their most honourable kings, Richard Coeur de Lion, had signed a document for its return to Scotland, but the merchants of London would not let it go . . . A reward of £2,000 was offered to informers, but had no more effect than a former offer of £30,000 for the person of Prince Charles Edward . . . Everyone hoped that his next door neighbour had it.'

Being a known Nationalist, Wendy Wood was the recipient of correspondence from a variety of bodies. *Brith*, the journal of the British Israelites, threatened that unless the Stone was returned at once to 'the King of Israel, George VI', all connected with the theft would be cursed. Her response was that 'God could be relied on to size up the situation in Scotland's favour.' The then Earl of Thomond in Ireland wrote her too. Claiming descent from Brian Boru, King of Ireland, and, as such, the rightful owner of the Irish Stone, the Lia Fail he named her Guardian of the Stone.

She was, of course, a suspect. In March, knowing the CID were after her, she stocked up her Moidart croft house and went to Glasgow hoping the CID would follow her and thus leave the croft as a safe haven for Stone carriers. She told MacCormick about a good underwater mooring for the Stone in her loch.

Long after the events of 1951, John Rollo made a secret recording in which he told the truth

10

about what happened after he had received the Stone. This was not released till after his death since when the BBC have used it on several occasions. In his clipped matter-of-fact Scots voice he tells how, at half-past-six on Hogmanay he was busy stock-taking in his Bonnybridge works. The phone rang. It was Bertie Gray asking how long he would be at the works— two people wanted to see him. Rollo promised to wait.

When they arrived, Gray told him the Stone of Destiny was in the car and asked would Rollo, as a good Scot, look after it for a time? Rollo agreed. They ran out to the Armstrong Siddeley. The Stone under its rug was still acting as the front seat. After cooking the young drivers a hearty meal, Rollo found himself left alone with the Stone.

Next morning— New Year's Day—Rollo returned to the empty factory, built a strong packing case and, using overhead gear, lifted the Stone into it. Removing the planking from a space beneath his foreman's office, he manoevered the case into it and sealed it with nails instantly rusted with sal-ammoniac. The press were soon on his tail, as his sympathies were known. About the 12th of January David Forrester, Secretary of the Covenant committee, phoned him late at night. Would he come over, urgently.

Rollo skidded through eight-inch snow to Bishopbriggs. Alan Stuart's father offered him an H.P. Sauce carton, containing Kay's portion of the Stone. He took it to his factory and stuck it in the kneehole of his desk. A bright young detective found names and addresses of three students on application slips at the Mitchell Library, Hamilton, Vernon and Stuart, but none of them knew where the evidence now was. The police haunted Rollo's factories around the Highlands, one of which had been built on the Matheson croft at Inverasdale, asking about

Wendy Wood

unusually heavy packing cases.

'A detective was sent from Glasgow,' says Kay, '— Calum Robertson— he had Gaelic. He thought nobody knew who he was, and he went and stayed with his relations at Sheildaig Lodge Hotel, who immediately phoned me to say it was him. He was going around, and all the folk knew that he was a Skye man, and what he was there for. And the yarns they were telling him! They had him away up at a loch in the hill, and he was buying them drams— they had the night of their lives— what a fool they made of him. His pocket was empty by the time he went off— and all for nothing.

'Another lot came questioning me, and I said — well if they wouldn't tell anyone, it was in the peat bank. And they started cutting the peats— I had all my peats cut! All the old bodachs, the old men, were saying 'you could have told us first and we'd have told them it was in our peat'. The old folk had a right good laugh'.

Rollo believed Scotland needed local employment, and Kay's mother offered the ex-army site on her croft. 'It was going until he died, which meant that there was four young families who didn't have to go away from the district, and one old man, which made a big difference in Inverasdale. He was a dedicated man. It's a pity there weren't more like him. There are Nationalists who are genuine, but not down to earth in a practical way like him'.

Eventually Rollo rented storage space for several large boxes of heavy goods from his old friend Tommy Smith, who ran David Goodfellow & Conear Stirling. With some difficulty he transported the heavy crate to Goodfellow's. His co-director, the late James Scott, put the HP Sauce carton in his garage.

Meanwhile Rollo said that Bertie Gray was keeping one or more than one, accurate reproductions of the Stone of Destiny in his monumental yard. Scotland Yard brought in a Dutch clairvoyant who saw the Stone lying in an old building alongside a river, beside a bridge, near an ancient church. The river ran through a capital city. Of course Scotland Yard only knew of two capital cities—London and Edinburgh. The Thames was searched as far upriver as Reading.

Goodfellows' factory— an old building— was on the Stirling side of the footbridge over to Cambuskenneth Abbey, alongside the Forth— which runs through Edinburgh. The clairvoyant had been astoundingly accurate. Towards the end of March MacCormick and Gray asked Rollo to hand over the Stone. He was reluctant to give it back until he knew and approved of what was going to happen to it.

But he had a special mason's handbarrow made by Stuart Henderson, a Perth coachbuilder. In Glasgow, after a dummy run with a bag of coal during which he was nearly caught by the police, he finally managed to deliver the Stone to the house of Willie White in respectable Bearsden. MacCormick and Gray were there with a mason. It was the evening of Easter Monday 1951. Rollo watched as the mason began to chisel holes for two brass dowels which would help to hold the repaired Stone together and knew his role as caretaker was over.

The next thing he saw was a newspaper picture of Arbroath Abbey, and a familiar-looking sandstone block draped in the Scottish flag. His voice was full of disgust as he told of the shameful way the Stone was abandoned at the High Altar, and of how the people in charge of it skulked away.

Wendy Wood takes up the tale. It is April 13th 1951. She is walking along a street in Dumbarton when a bus conductor shouted to her that the Stone was now in Forfar Police station. She rushed to Glasgow, collected fifteen students, threw them onto train to Forfar— where they missed the removal of the Stone by twenty

above Ian Hamilton *right* Councillor Bertie Gray

minutes, as it sped to Glasgow Central Police Station. 'The English did not dare to prosecute the raiders,' she writes, 'even when at last they knew who they were.'

Then the rumours started up again. Was it the same Stone that had been brought from Westminster? If not— who had it? In the mid sixties a mysterious Stone turned up in Parliament Square, Edinburgh. The Revd John Mackay Nimmo, a staunch Nationalist, Minister of St Columba's Church in Dundee, Chaplain to the Knights of St John, recalls that he was asked if he would be prepared to take this Stone into Sanctuary. 'We had a service attended by Nationalists from all over Scotland and we accepted the Stone. Baillie Gray was at this service and there he assured me that this was the real Stone of Destiny. It was well known in the town, one of the landmarks of the place. The very night the Stone came here the Chief Constable of Dundee said he'd heard that I had stolen property in my church. 'Well,' I said, 'this is true. But it is a question of who had stolen it.' In the morning he said 'I've been in touch with the authorities— I presume he meant at Westminster— and they said that they had their Stone and they were happy with it. We had our Stone and he was happy about that.'

Dr Hugh Ryan, one of the Stone's historians, firmly believed that the one in Westminster Abbey was genuine. With a laugh and a sniff so you don't know if he's serious, he talked on another old recording about his friend Bertie Gray, saying how he wouldn't trust him, that his stories were doubtful. He even told the police not to believe Gray because of his mischievous Scots sense of humour and his fondness for deliberately creating mysteries.

But questions about the provenance of the Stone went on. Historian Archie McKerracher, writing in the eighties, said: 'Bertie Gray made two copies; one in 1928 and one in 1950. I think that the 1950 copy is now the stone in Westminster Abbey beneath the Coronation chair. The 1928 copy which wasn't quite as accurate is in the church in Dundee, and the Westminster Stone is at a secret location in the Arbroath area . . . it is produced on certain occasions and taken through the streets of Arbroath. I don't think the Westminster people, having got a stone back, were going to quibble.'

Gray, before sealing the join in the Stone, dug out a little space and filled it with a piece of paper on which he had written 'This Stone was stolen by Edward 1 in 1296 and it should be returned to Scotland'. The crumbs he divided between those involved in the taking.

Ten years later he is saying in a newspaper interview, 'Oh I can't really be sure which Stone I sent back to London— there were so many copies lying about.' Ryan said quizzically that, while Gray loved a chance to take the mickey out of the credulous English, he later told Nimmo that he was giving him the real Stone. Frank J. Dimes of London, Chief Scientific Officer of the

above Cambuskenneth Abbey; *opposite* The Stone on Rollo's handbarrow discovered at Arbroath Abbey on April 13, 1951

Institute of Geological Sciences, tried to identify the returned stone through minute inspection. He found it did contain pea-sized volcanic pebbles, not unlike those he had noted in the original. He thought that it was highly unlikely that a piece of stone so exactly similar could have been found. But he said there was no doubt now that the Stone of Scone had been quarried in eastern Perthshire not far from Scone. Of course any sculptor worth his sporran would have gone to Perthshire for raw materials for his spoof rock— there's plenty left where the Stone of Scone came from, containing matching volcanic pebbles. Scientists are now capable of finding brass dowels inside blocks of stone without damaging them, but Westminster responds to requests: 'Under no circumstances will you be permitted to carry out any form of test, electronic or othewise, on the Stone'.

Ian Hamilton believes Westminster has the real Stone of Scone. Rollo's daughter Margaret maintains that the stone her father looked after is the one that went back to Westminster. But Kay Matheson, who is in no doubt about her views, (I most definitely didn't think it should be given back to England) says of the Westminster authorities: 'Well— if it's the real Stone they got back . . .' her voice tails off, but her eyes twinkle with mischief.

Wendy Wood wrote 'It was a piece of sophistry that still makes one blink . . . The Stone, we were told, was no use hidden. It could not much longer remain undetected, and it was better to give it up than have it taken.' Some thought that if the authorities dared to snatch the Stone back to England, they would outrage Scottish feeling, perhaps motivating them sufficiently to push for change.

Wood was not yet done with the Stone. In 1968 she 'went to the Abbey and slipped a piece of cardboard under the complicated iron railings (as high as a deer fence) on which was printed,

This is not the original Stone of Destiny. The real real Stone is of black basalt marked with hieroglyphics and is inside a hill in Scotland'. 'I stood and enjoyed . . . the grovellings of the officials as they tried to get any part of their anatomy under their own wrought iron restrictions. As there is a lens in the middle of a Tudor rose in the chapel opposite, which automatically registers anything that passes the railing, I wondered what comic cuts were perhaps being produced.'

A brief diary of what happened to the returned stone is noted in the Westminster copy of Hamilton's book, ending 'Kept in vault, replaced in Chair 26th Feb 1952'.

And there, it would seem, the story of the Stone ends. Or does it?

3. Queens, Kings and Coronation Chairs

Why is it that so much angst is expended on a dusty old piece of sandstone which is only brought into use for occasional ceremonies?

Inauguration ceremonies and coronations have been evolving since the earliest times. The pharaohs wore crowns to symbolise royal rank. In ancient Greece and Rome athletes and poets were crowned with wreaths in recognition of public service. David was crowned and anointed King of Israel, and the early Church, believing him to be the forefather of all kings, copied his ceremony for coronations. Since the 14th century the Catholic Church has also bestowed the Tiara— a triple crown— upon its Popes.

In England, coronation requires the populace to give its public consent. An oath is sworn by the sovereign to govern according to certain requirements. Also there is consecration by the Church through prayer and anointment; investiture with the regalia which symbolically clothe the monarch in the office of sovereignty; enthronement which places her in the seat of government, and communion to seal the pact with God.

But Scottish monarchs were inaugurated on a quite different set of principles. Professor Duncan, of Glasgow University's Department of Scottish History, explains that stones have been used since the earliest times: 'It is undoubtedly an ancient ritual, seating a ruler down as the symbol of inauguration. Throughout the Indo-European world the seating of man and woman, formally side by side, was a form of marriage, and similarly the seating of a ruler upon something is a symbol of his marriage to the people and perhaps in ancient times to the goddess of the people.'

This practice is first recorded in 800 AD, with Charlemagne, whose *Marmorne Stuhl* or marble chair can still be seen at Aix-la-Chapelle in France. It is a plain heavy seat of white marble mounted on five steps. At coronations it was covered with gold. Stone was also used in Ireland, where the new king would place his foot in the footprint of his predecessor as he took the various oaths. This footprint was most usually gouged out of 'living' rock— that is, outcrop rock which is part of the underlying geological structure. Occasionally footprints are also found on movable boulders. Could it be that these ancient people thought the basic elements of life on the planet, sun, water, and stone, made reliable witnesses to promises and vows? Certainly stone has been used as a witness to human activity since the earliest times, from Jacob in the Book of Genesis to the Standing Stones we see in northern Europe, and to beautiful Pictish carvings like Sueno's Stone by the Moray Firth. We still bear witness to the lives of our loved ones by placing a headstone above their graves.

Since the coronation of Edward II at Westminster Abbey in 1308, the English church has brought together the notions of inauguration on stone and of the biblical way of crowning a monarch. For a time the anointing, investiture and crowning of the Sovereign were private ceremonies, carried out by the Lords Spiritual, and taking place on the Coronation Chair in the Sanctuary of the Abbey. Monarchs were required to strip to the waist for the anointing, and then had to grovel before the High Altar.

For the public and secular part of the ceremony, carried out by the Lords Temporal, a throne was set on a stage beneath the Crossing so that all present could see their monarch. From this throne the newly crowned monarch received homage from the people.

In the present century British Coronations have become more elaborate. They are consist of four sections: THE INTRODUCTION—the Archbishop of Canterbury ushers in the sovereign and presents her to the assembled throng, extracting from her a promise to govern according to law. THE ANOINTING is done on the Coronation Chair, under a canopy held by four Knights of the Garter. Holy oil is poured into a spoon through the beak of a gold eagle. The Archbishop anoints the sovereign's head, hands and breast while the choir sings 'Zadok the priest'. Zadok was priest to King David of Israel, and to the young King Solomon, from whom all monarchs including the English ones are supposed to descend and through whom they once claimed their Divine Right to govern. THE INVESTITURE involves the Sovereign being dressed in white linen and cloth of gold, and given spurs, a sword, an orb, ring, the sceptre symbolising power and justice, and a rod with a dove on it symbolising equity and mercy. Finally the Archbishop places the crown on her head. While the present crown is not very old, it is said to contain the original crown of Edward the Confessor (r.1042- 66), a

contemporary of the Scottish king, Macbeth. In England ancient objects are revered just as they are in Scotland. THE ENTHRONEMENT comes after the people acclaim their new sovereign by expressing their approval in loud cheers before they pay homage to her.

Edward II was the first English king to be crowned in the Coronation Chair which, admits the *Westminster Abbey Official Guide*, his father ordered 'to enclose the famous Stone of Scone, which he seized in 1296 and brought from Scotland to the Abbey'. This Stone weighed 990 kilos (four hundredweight), and Edward I had iron rings fixed to each side for its journey south. Since then it has been used by every monarch. Oliver Cromwell also thought its magic necessary for his installation as Lord Protector.

In Scotland, inaugurations of early *Ardrigh*, provincial kings of areas such as *Dalriada* (Argyll), in the early years just after the Romans had left Britain, were simple affairs by comparison. Picture the scene: close to the *Ardrigh*, with his right foot planted in the excised footprint on the stone of honour at the summit of Dunadd Hill, stands the *Righdomna* or *Tanist*, the heir-apparent of the monarchy, who has been nominated according to the fundamental Celtic principle of shared authority. Pictish kings were elective, and this theory pervaded all the institutions of the Gaelic people, who chose not only their clan chiefs, their *Ardrigh*, but also the supreme ruler of their nation in this way.

When Scots reached the stage of having one overall king, around the ninth century, they inaugurated him by sitting him on a bare Stone in the open air. As the centuries wore on they began to drape the Stone with silk, dressing it up more and more till eventually, by the thirteenth century, as we can see from evidence in the old royal seals, they had enshrined it in a chair made of elaborately carved wood. Where else did Edward I get the idea of placing the stone he

Coronation Chair with Sugarloaf Stone

having there placed him in the regal chair, decked with silk cloths embroidered with gold, the Bishop of St Andrews, the others assisting him, consecrated him king, the king himself sitting, as was proper, upon the regal chair [that is, the stone] and the earls and other nobles placing vestments under his feet, with bent knees, before the stone.

'This stone is reverently preserved in that monastery for the consecration of kings of Scotland; nor were any of the kings in wont to reign anywhere in Scotland, unless they had, on receiving the name of the king, first sat upon this royal stone in Scone, which was constituted by ancient kings the *sedes superior* or principal seat, that is to say, of Albania.

Two features of the English ceremony are absent in this inauguration: there is neither anointing nor crowning. In fact no Scottish king was either crowned or anointed until the fourteenth century, after Robert the Bruce had successfully applied to the Pope for recognition of Scotland as an individual nation in its own right, separate from England. The first Scottish king to be crowned and anointed was David II, in 1329.

Professor Duncan doubts that the Stone was ever itself a ritual object. His theory is that it was the sitting of the person rather than the actual seat that mattered. But he agrees that when Robert the Bruce was inaugurated, some other type of stone was used, for we are told that he sat on 'the kingis stole [stool].' He does not doubt that the use of a stone goes back for hundreds of years before we hear of it and possibly even for a thousand or more.

One problem in all this is the fluidity of opinion and prejudice and the paucity of hard historical evidence.

took from Scone in 1296 inside the coronation chair?

The first documented Scottish inauguration is that of Alexander III, in 1249, described by an Aberdeen chantry priest, John of Fordoun, thus:

Alexander . . . a boy of eight years old, came to Scone . . . on . . . Tuesday, the 13th of July. There were present the venerable fathers David de Bernham, Bishop of St Andrews, and Galfridus, Bishop of Dunkeld . . . the Abbott of the same monastery of Scone . . . [They] led the future King Alexander to the cross, which stands in the *cimiterium* or churchyard at the east end of the church; and,

PART II

4. How the Legend Began

For some, legend and myth will always mean fairytales, even lies, but for others they represent the efforts made by human beings to make sense of things that once actually happened. Increasingly, historians and anthropologists are finding useful sources of information in these traditional stories, and sometimes vital clues, which can start archaeologists on trails that lead to discovery of fascinating pieces of the jig-saw that makes up our past. Every few years evidence turns up which corroborates some ancient myth. New methods of detection develop. Dowsers and clairvoyants are employed because they see what science is as yet incapable of discovering. It may be that all the clues we need to find the Stone are there for the taking—if only we could recognise them.

For hundreds of years the stories about the Stone of Destiny remained flexibly in the oral tradition of Scotland. Hardly anyone felt the need to write them down. Folklore grows best in a compost of memories, misunderstandings and wishful thinking. In order for it to flourish and endure, however, it must be animated with the spirit of some real human value, and it must be rooted—however far back—in fact. Storyteller Duncan Williamson was born into an non-literate culture in which you learned by listening, observing and remembering. Aged fifteen he took to the road himself, in the best possible

position to understand the organic quality of story, and how it mutates according to its audience. In the absence of written records, Scots owe an enormous debt to people like Williamson and the ballad-singers, and to those who collect their lore, like Dr Hamish Henderson of the School of Scottish Studies in Edinburgh...

History shows us that the British regard the Stone of Destiny as a talisman. Folklore tells us how and why—for its magical and protective powers over the Scots. Modern journalism notes that the authorities at Westminster hang on to the Stone in spite of the many treaties England has made promising its return.

The legend comes down to us in spoken and in written form and some of the early writers used written sources that have since disappeared. Each of the accounts varies in detail and spellings change too, but parts of the story and many names remain consistent. Only by working through their complexities can we see how the story grew.

The Victorians took an interest in the Stone. In 1866 Joseph Robertson of the Register House, Edinburgh, enumerated a few facts he had gleaned from Scottish Chronicles, written at various periods from the tenth century, which showed that at least as early as AD 906 Scone was a royal city, the meeting place of a national council or assembly, and Scottish kings were

Duncan Williamson

crowned there *super Cathedram Regadem lapideam* (on a royal stone chair). The oldest writer who tells the legend of the Royal Stone is William of Rishanger, who lived until after 1327, and who describes the coronation in 1292 of king John Balliol at Scone, *super lapidem Regadem* (on a royal stone). Robertson also cites Andrew of Wyntoun, a prior of St Serf's in Loch Leven who wrote a *Metrical Chronicle of Scotland* about 1424, in which Simon Brek's father, the king of Spain, gave him 'a gret Stane that for thei Kygis sete was made' and bade him take it to Ireland:

And wyn that land and occupy,
And halde that Stane perpetually,
And make it his sege Stane
As thai of Spayne did of it ane.

Robertson also argued that there must have been two Stones at Scone, believing that, while Edward 1 took 'the Stone of Fate' to Westminster, yet there remained at Scone 'a Stone Chair, in which it would seem the Stone of Fate was placed when kings were to be inaugurated . . . in 1306 we read that king Robert Bruce was placed in the Royal Seat at Scone. So also king Robert II . . . we have record of his sitting next day in the Royal Seat on the Moothill of Scone.'

The earliest written version of the Stone of Destiny legend discovered in recent times is quoted by English folklorist Jennifer Westwood in her book *Albion* (1985). It comes from a monk, Robert of Gloucester (1230-1300), who traces the first Irish immigrations. He says

[they] broghte into Scotland a whyte marble
ston,
Zat was ordeyned for hure kyng, whan he
coroned wer.
And for a grete Jewyll long hit was yholde
ther.

Westwood suggests that Edward 1 took it to England 'because he was a superstitious man who fully believed in the power of the *Fatale*

Marmor . . . the Stone of Fate. For the stone was invested with mana . . . it very likely *did* come from Ireland with the Scots'. She reminds us that the custom of using stone 'had to do with the cult of the ancestor, whose spirits perhaps dwelt in the stone, so that the newly invested king received the 'luck' or mana of his predecessors by contact with it'. In Norway kings were enthroned on the burial mounds of their forebears, probably with similar reasoning.

The Victorian Professor William Skene examined the documentary evidence:

Hector Boece wrote the *Scotorum Historiae* in 1537, in which 'Gaythelus, a Greek, the son either of the Athenian Cecrops or the Argive Neolus, went to Egypt' at the time of the Exodus, where he married Scota, the daughter of Pharao, and after the destruction of the Egyptian army in the Red Sea, fled with her by the Mediterranenan till he arrived in Portingall, where he landed, and founded a kingdom at Brigantium, now Compostella. Here he reigned in the marbile chair, which was the '*lapis fatalis cathedrae instar*', or fatal stone like a chair, and wherever it was found portended kingdom to the Scots . . . Simon Breck, a descendant of Gathelus, brought the chair from Spain to Ireland, and was crowned in it as King of Ireland . . . Fergus, son of Ferchard, was first King of the Scots in Scotland, and brought the chair from Ireland to Argyll, and was crowned in it. He built a town in Argyll called Beregonium, in which he placed it . . The twelfth king, Evenus, built a town near Beregonium, called after his name Evonium, now called Dunstaffnage, to which the stone was removed . . . ' Eventually Fergus Mac Erc 'is crowned in the marble chair. He builds a church at Iona, and commands it to be the sepulchre of the kings in future.

The *Scalacronica*, compiled in 1355, begins with Simon Brec, youngest son of the King of Spain, bringing to Ireland 'a stone on which the kings of Spain were wont to be crowned'. Brec 'placed it in the most sovereign beautiful place in Ireland, called to this day the Royal Place [Tara], and Fergus, son of Ferchar, brought the royal stone before received, and placed it where is now the Abbey of Scone'. Here the Stone moves directly from Ireland to Scone.

The earliest history of Scotland, the *Scotichronon*, by Fordun, who was alive in 1386, is a little thinner. He says Gaythelus married a Pharaoh's daughter, Scota, and led those who weren't drowned in the Red Sea through Africa to Spain. A Spanish king descended from him sent his son, Simon Brec, to Ireland, presenting him with 'the *Marmorea Cathedra*, the marble chair, diligently and carefully sculptured by ancient art, on which the kings of Spain, of Scottish race were wont to sit'. This stone chair he placed in Tara, 'the royal seat and principal place of the kingdom of Ireland'. Fordun quotes the '*Ni fallat fatum* prophecy and says that Fergus, who led the Scots from Ireland to Scotland, brought with him 'the royal chair cut out of marble stone, in which he was crowned first king there by the Scots, after whose example the succeeding kings received the rite of coronation in the same chair'.

Skene sums up the 'facts' he has gleaned from these pieces of evidence; 'It is true that such a stone was preserved at Scone; it is true that Scottish monarchs were crowned upon it; and it is true that in 1296 Edward 1 removed it to Westminster Abbey, where it now is, and can be seen under the seat of the Coronation Chair.' Nowadays we may have reason to cast doubts on the accuracy of some of these 'truths.'

When Fordun, who died less than a hundred years after Alexander III, wrote that the young king sat 'as was proper, upon the regal chair—that is, the stone', the folk-memory was still fresh. It is known that he collected some of his information from sources now lost to us and we can feel reasonably happy that his account was accurate—there was indeed a special stone used in the king-making ceremony at Scone. Rishanger, an English annalist, wrote in his *Chronica et Annales* (1327), 'John de Balioll. . . (collocatus super lapidem regadem)—placed upon the regal stone—which Jacob placed under his head when he went from Bersabee to Haran, was solemnly crowned . . . at Scone'. He had no particular reason to lie, so again we can probably take it as a fact that the Stone was still in use in 1292 at Balliol's inauguration. But when Rishanger goes on to say that Edward 1 'passed by the Abbey of Scone, where having taken away the stone which the Kings of Scotland were wont at the time of their coronation to use for a throne, carried it to Westminster'. (The original Latin reads: '*ubi sublato lapide quo Reges Scotorum, tempore cor onationis, solebant uti pro throno, usque Westmonasterium transtulit illum, jubens inde fieri celebrantium cathedram sacerdotum*') Many historians now cast doubts on his accuracy, for reasons which may become apparent later on.

The second earliest written source of information comes in the form of two extant manuscripts of what at first appears to be a poem, written after the death of Edward 1 in 1307.

LA PIERRE D'ESCOCE

Qei est la piere de Escoce, vous die pur verite,
Sur qei les Roys d'Escoce estoint mis en see.
Johan Balol le drein fust, a ceo q'est counte,
Qe sur cests piere resceut sa dignite.

Ore l'ad conquise Edward Roy d'Engleterre,
Par la grace Jhesu Criste et par forte guere.
A Seint Edward la present com roy de graunt affaire.
Ore est passe par la morte que nul ne poet retrere

En Egipte Moise a le poeple precha,
Scota la file Faraon bien l'escota,
Qare il dite en espirite, 'Qe ceste piere avera,
De molt estraunge terre conquerour serra.

Gaidelons et Scota cest piere menerount
Quant de la terre Egipte en Escose passerount,
Ne geres loyns de Scone quant ariveront.
De la noun de Scota la Escose terre numount.

Puis la mort la Scota son baron femme ne prist,
Mais en la terre de Galway sa demore fist.
De son noune demoisne le noune de Galway mist.
Issi pert qe pare lour nouns Escose et Galway ist.

Ore est Edward passe hors de ceste vie,
Conquerour de terres, la flour de chivalrie,
Prioms Dieu omnipotent, qe tout le moundeguye,
Qe Dieu de s'alme eyt mercy, Dieu le fitz Marye.

The late Dominica Legge, Reader in French at Edinburgh University, translated it and made a detailed study of the work, proving it was once in fact a song:

'What the Stone of Scotland is, I tell you for truth, on which the Kings of Scotland were placed in their seat. John Baliol was the last, according to what is told, who received his dignity on this stone.

'Now Edward King of Englad has conquered it, by the grace of Jesus Christ and by hard warfare. He offers it to St Edward like a king of great importance. Now he has passed by death, that no one can avoid.

'In Egypt Moses preached to the people. Scota, Pharoah's daughter, listened well, for he said in the spirit, 'Whoso will possess this stone, shall be the conqueror of a very far-off land.'

'Gaidelon and Scota brought this stone, when they passed from the land of Egypt to Scotland, not far from Scone, when they arrived. They named the land Scotland from Scota's name.

'After Scota's death her husband took no other wife, but made his dwelling in the land of Galloway. From his own name he gave Galloway its name. Thus it appears that Scotland and Galloway are derived from their names.

'Now has Edward passed from this life, the conqueror of lands and flower of chivalry. Let us pray almighty God, who sways the whole world, that God may have mercy on his soul, God the son of Mary.'

Here, Scota and her husband go directly from Egypt to Scone without stopping off in Spain, Ireland or Argyll, all of which appear in later versions of the legend. Legge explains that the manuscripts may be abbreviated versions of the story, because the original is known to have been quarried along with other material for somewhat creative versions of history. Robertson has explained how 'events which may have really happened are frequently misplaced and transferred to a wrong epoch, very often owing their misplacement to a wish to build up the fame of some favourite hero, by attributing to him the merit of every important action of several different periods. Scottish history abounds with in stances of such misplacement'. The irrelevant detail that Gaidelon remained a widower after Scota's death suggests that the original source for *La Piere D'Escoce* was much fuller. The style in which the poem is set out was rare after the 12th century in England, and so may in fact be a cut-down version of a much older lyric. She reminds us that its version of Moses' prophecy is corroborated in another 14th century English manuscript—the *Vita Edwardi II.*

One of the oldest written references to the Stone comes from the time of Robert the Bruce. In 1301 the Scottish government was in direct competition with England for help from the Vatican. Desperate for recognition as an independent state, it commissioned the learned Canon Baldred Bisset of St Andrews to write up the history of Scotland in such a way as to 'prove' to Pope Boniface VIII that Scots had been converted to Christianity four centuries before the English, and that they had been civilised throughout the reigns of thirty-six kings while the English were still pagan. With this aim, Bisset set out a historical justification for the ancient right of Scotland to freedom from domination and presented it in Rome and, while Edward 1 was attempting to convince the bewildered Boniface that whilst Scots descended from Alberactus, the *youngest* son of Brutus (the *Eponymus* of the Britons) the English came from the eldest and were therefore of greater importance. Canon Bisset was explaining how the daughter of Pharaoh, along with some Irish, had sailed to Scotland, taking with her the royal seat which Edward had carried away by violence to England. He accused Edward of taking other significant items as well. The Canon further said that Scota conquered and destroyed the Picts and took and named their kingdom, tactfully massaging history into a more acceptable story, editing out an embarrassing expulsion of the Britons (English) by early Scots and blaming the Picts. It worked. Pope Boniface preferred Baldred's story. Skene, who was not above adding and subtracting from history himself, says the whole story was fabricated. But would Canon Bisset actually have endangered his immortal soul by lying to the head of his Church?

Because these early accounts, written independently of each other, have some common features, Legge argues that Bisset did not invent his story, as Skene suggested, 'but that a fairly extensive form of it was current in the thirteenth century.

Another Victorian historian, Hemingford, wrote: 'At the Monastery of Scone was placed a large stone in the church of God, near the great altar, hollowed out like a round chair, in which future kings were placed, according to custom, as the place of their coronation (in Latin: *Apud Monasterium de Scone positus erat lapis pergrandis in ecclesia Dei, juxta manum altare, concavus quidem ad modum rotundae cathedreaie confectus, in quo future reges loco quasi coronationis ponebantur ex more*).' This gave rise to the theory that the Stone of Destiny might once have been a Roman altar—a theory which will be examined later. Skene's research, 'Among the king's jewels which were in the castle of Edinburgh in 1296, was *una petra magna super quam Reges Scotiae solebant coronari* (a great stone upon which Scottish Kings were crowned) suggested, on the contrary, that the original Stone must still be in Edinburgh, because the Westminster Stone is so small.

We all read between the lines when we read history, adding and subtracting according to our degree of scepticism, making links according to our knowledge. Amateur historian Archie McKerracher accuses Skene of turning 'academic somersaults' in order to prove Queen Victoria had been rightfully crowned on the Stone. McKerracher is particularly knowledgeable about the Perthshire area and has long been interested in legends about the Stone. He has looked at how it became known as the Stone of Destiny, blaming misunderstanding on the part of translators for theories such as that the Stone of Destiny was *Lia Fail*, the Oracle Stone used at the coronation of the Irish high kings which, in fact, 'remained on Tara Hill until 1798'. Like historians before him, he theorises: the name 'Destiny' has come down to us 'due to a series of errors', the prophecy

'*Ni fallat fatum, Scoti quocunque locatum
Invenient lapidem, regnare tenatur ibidem*'.

was incorrectly copied by Boece from Fordun—instead of the noun *fatum* Boece wrote '*fatalis*', and Bellenden, who later translated this 'for James V who couldn't read Latin', expressed *fatalis* (badly) as 'fateful'—hence 'fatal' and 'fateful'. McKerracher suggests 'The Gaelic word *faileas* means a spiritual shadow . . . it is the merest slip of a pen, or a mis-hearing, to render that as *fail*—meaning fateful . . . From that somebody derived 'Destiny'. In the 16th century the prophecy read:

'The Scottis sall bruke
that realme as native ground
Gif weirdes (fates) faill nocht,
quhairevir this chiar is found'.

McKerracher discusses also the apparently nonsensical translation made by 'a gentleman' of the words found on one of the plaques discovered much later in Macbeth's Castle, and floats the suggestion that 'the dying Bruce had entrusted the Stone to Angus Og of the Isles to save it from the Balliols . . . One tradition says it lies in a cave behind a waterfall on Skye and the location is known today only to a family of MacDonalds, descendants of Angus Og, who are its hereditary custodians'.

The legend grows. McKerracher, like Skene, Boece, Fordun and the amiable Baldred Bisset, sifts nuggets from history, stirs in some educated guesswork, and produces tasty morsels of folk-lore. Through it comes breathing the spirit of the people. Why has the legend persisted? Because it is boiled up from the bones of ancient fact.

The facts are these: early peoples did travel from Israel to Spain and Ireland. They used stones as ballast for their boats, which were capable of carrying quite heavy cargo, including large stone objects. There was a special Stone on which Kings of Scots were crowned. It was kept near the altar at Scone Abbey. It was extremely large. It had some kind of shaping, with a concave top. It was carved in some way. Edward 1 did take a block, cut from Perthshire sandstone, to Westminster in 1296.

Another contemporary historian, Marion Campbell, notes in her book *Argyll, the Enduring Heartland* (1977) 'Legend will even tackle geological oddities; volcanic bubbles in a rock-sheet on the north shore of Loch Crinan have been explained as the hoof-marks of the horse on which Scota . . . rode ashore, bearing with her (as Nennius records) Jacob's Pillow'.

Legends are quarried by writers of fiction, and the first appearance of the Stone story being used in this way is *Scottish Chiefs* (1810), a charming little novel about William Wallace by an English-woman, Miss Jane Porter. Quoth her Earl of Monteith: 'the hallowed pillar [i.e. the Stone] was taken from Scone by the command of the king of England . . . The archives of the kingdom have also been torn from their sanctuary and were thrown by Edward's own hands into the fire.' Wallace responds, 'Scotland's history is in the memories of her sons; her palladium is in

their hearts; and Edward may one day find that she . . . needs not talismans to give her freedom'. He is then entrusted with an unusually heavy box—does it contain the Stone? Porter's footnote explains: 'Iber the Phoenician, who came from the Holy Land to inhabit the coast of Spain, brought this sacred relic along with him. From Spain he transplanted it with the colony he sent to people the south of Ireland; and from Ireland it was brought into Scotland by the great Fergus, the son of Ferchard. He placed it in Argyleshire; but Mac Alpine removed it to Scone, and fixed it in the royal chair in which all the succeeding kings of Scotland were inaugurated. Edward I of England caused it to be carried to Westminster Abbey where it now stands. The tradition is that empire abides where it stays.'

Letters appear, written by people who mix vague memories of 1950-51 with scraps of history. The uncharitable might call them garbled tales. Actually they contain seeds of a new folklore which are being sown in the minds of the next generation. The story of Scota and Gaythelus may be the folklore of How the Scots and the Gaels Got Their Names, but it is interesting to note how persistently certain parts of their story turn up, and from diverse sources. Simon Brec, not a particularly Spanish name, turns up with particular frequency.

We don't like gaping holes in stories so, instinctively, we fill them in with invented reasons, driven to answer questions with suppositions, creative conclusions which the listener re-tells as truth. This need to link parts of a story provides the mesh upon which legend embroiders itself into such a winsome tapestry. Facts themselves are prone to interpretation—one has only to look at the way in which the Bible, which purports to be Truth, has been used. History is a magnificent quiz-show in which everyone can join.

5. Jacob and the Thunderstones

Every legend about the Stone begins by saying that it was the pillow on which Jacob had his dream.

Jacob, grandson of Abraham, lived around 1700 BC. At that time, explains Dr Graham Durant, Curator of Mineralogy and Petrology at the Hunterian Museum, Glasgow, meteorites were 'believed to be very special'. The Greeks called them 'Thunder Stones' and most early peoples believed they had supernatural powers. Two kinds of meteorites hurtle towards us, from the asteroid belt between Mars and Jupiter, as shooting stars which hit the earth's surface with crater-making impact, the friction of their passage through the atmosphere melting a smooth crust around the stony *aerolites*, reducing *siderites* into petrified splashes of metal. 'There was little understanding of anything being outside the earth other than heaven,' Durant explains how early peoples regarded them. 'Only in the 18th century were scientists able to explain their true origin.' Meteorites are either 'finds' or 'falls'. Many 'finds' turn out to be basalts with weathered crusts—not meteorites at all. 'There's an example of polished basalt in the Black Chair here in the museum.'

The Stone of Destiny is supposed to have been covered with carvings. If it was a meteorite, I asked Dr Durant, would people living between the era of Solomon (960 BC) and that of Columba (563 AD) have had the technology to work on it? He explained that following the hypothesis that Jacob's pillow was described as 'stone' it must have been silicate—no different from normal rock. But aren't meteorites usually quite small—about the size of a tennis ball? 'Yes,' agrees Durant, 'but they are occasionally huge.' In the eighteenth century a Russian blacksmith found one weighing 1600 lbs, which would have measured about three cubic feet and in Thracia in 476 BC a Thunder Stone as large as a chariot fell. It is at least possible, then, that Jacob found a suitably sized meteorite for his pillow, upon which marks of some kind could have been carved.

Are there any precedents connecting meteorites and religion? The early Arabs worshipped gods who were thought to reside in sacred stones, trees and other elements of nature. The city of Mecca has always been their spiritual home, containing its famous building, the Kaaba (cube).

In the eastern wall of the Kaaba, about five feet from the ground, a Black Stone is set. It is an aerolite which, well before the time of Muhummad, flashed through the sky and landed near an encampment of Arabs. They then made it an object of reverence. Muhummad was born around 570 AD into a clan of the Quraish tribe, Bedouins who ruled Mecca and had custodian ship of the Kaaba and its Stone.

Stone was used in Israel to mark special places. It could withstand desert storms, great heat and great cold. Being heavy, it could not easily be stolen or displaced.

The honour Jacob gave to his pillow-stone shines through King James V1's translation of the Old Testament. In Genesis 28, Jacob was travelling from Beer-sheba to Haran when, at sunset,

(he) 'took of the stones of that place, and put them for his pillows, and lay down in that place to sleep. And he dreamed, and behold a ladder set up on the earth, and the top of it reached to heaven: and behold the angels of God ascending and descending on it. And, behold, the Lord stood above it, and said, I am the Lord god of Abraham thy father, and the God of Isaac: the land whereon thou liest, to thee will I give it, and to thy seed; And thy seed shall be as the dust of the earth, and thou shalt spread abroad to the west, and to the east, and to the north, and to the south . . . And Jacob awaked out of his sleep, and he said, Surely the Lord is in this place; and I knew it not . . . This is none other but the house of God, and this is the gate of heaven.

'And Jacob rose up early in the morning, and took the stone that he had put for his pillows, and set it up for a pillar, and poured oil upon the top of it. And he called the name of that place Beth-el . . . And Jacob vowed a vow, saying . . . this stone, which I have set for a pillar, shall be God's house.'

Jacob set his pillar up as a permanent landmark, so that he would recognise the place, and in pouring oil on it he was making a sacrifice. Stones continued to be important to him. At a well covered by 'a great stone' which he helped his cousin Rachel, a pretty shepherdess move, he fell in love with her and thus began a polygamous relationship with his uncle's family and their servants that was to start a dynasty. Rachel produced a son, Joseph.

Twenty-two years later God told Jacob to return to Beth-el, where he re-named him Israel and said 'a company of nations shall be of thee, and kings shall come out of thy loins; And the land which I gave Abraham and Isaac, to thee I will give it, and to thy seed after thee.' Jacob's response again is to celebrate by setting up a stone pillar and making a sacrifice.

Soon after, near Bethlehem, Rachel went into

An aerolite landed in High Possil, Glasgow in 1804

a difficult labour. Another son, Benjamin, was born—but Rachel died. 'Jacob set a pillar upon her grave', marking it with a stone 'that is the pillar of Rachel's grave unto this day'. At Shechem, towards the end of his life, Jacob told his twelve sons, some of whom had turned out better than others, that each would start one of the tribes of Israel, giving Zebulun charge of the seaboard, and Dan the power of judgement. Yet in Judges 5, Deborah the prophetess asks 'Why did Dan remain in ships?' suggesting that it was Dan who went to sea. Jacob entrusted Joseph with custody of 'The stone of Israel'.

Later Joshua, the successor of Moses, called his tribes together in Shechem, to make a new law, and he 'took a great stone, and set it up there under an oak, that was by the sanctuary of the Lord. And Joshua said unto all the people, 'Behold, this stone shall be a witness unto us; for it hath heard all the words of the Lord which he spake unto us: it shall be therefore a witness unto you, lest ye deny your God.' Shortly after this, he died, reputedly aged a hundred and ten. The Pillar Stone was again used as a witness in 2 Kings 23 when King Josiah 'stood by a pillar, and made a covenant' that he would be good to his people.

Stone was believed capable of witnessing important events—of hearing the spoken word.

The Shechem stone next appears in Judges 9, when a character called Abimelech murdered seventy of his brothers and was rewarded when 'all the men of Shechem gathered together . . . and made Abimelech king by the plain of the pillar that was in Shechem'. After a plot that makes Macbeth look like a bed-time story, and in which the local trees are driven to emulate Abimelech by voting for the bramble to rule them, a woman sensibly dropped a stone on his head from a tower.

The men of Judah 'anointed David king' over them in 2 Samuel 2, about 1,000 BC, and the following chapter refers to 'the throne of David' being set up over Israel. When David lay dying, in 1 Kings 1, he ordered Zadok the priest and Nathan the Prophet to bring his son Solomon and 'anoint him there king over Israel . . . that he may come and sit upon my throne; for he shall be king in my stead.' Zadok duly anointed him with holy oil and all the people celebrated the fact that 'Solomon sitteth on the throne of the kingdom.' We are told unequivocally 'Then sat Solomon upon the throne of David his father; and his kingdom was established greatly'. We read of this again in 1 Chronicles 29 'Solomon sat on the throne of the Lord as King.' In this way, the practices of enthronement and anointing were established and as we have seen in chapter xx still taken with the same degree of seriousness by the British today, and treated with the same pomp and circumstance.

About 950 BC Solomon built a beautiful house for himself of stone, wood and gold, in 1 Kings 6, 'with carved figures of cherubims and palm trees and open flowers, and overlaid them with gold fitted upon the carved work.' The art of carving stone had been practiced already for hundreds of years for the inscription of laws, as on the pillar of King Hammurabi of Babylon (c1800 BC).

Was stone ever used in Biblical coronations? 2 Kings 11 has seven year-old Joash being brought secretly to the Temple in Jerusalem by Jehoiada the priest. With guards surrounding the place 'he brought forth the king's son and put the crown upon him . . . and they made him king, and anointed him; and they clapped their hands, and said, God save the king . . . and . . . behold, the king stood by a pillar, as the manner was'. Other translators have given 'stood on a pillar'. Whichever place is chosen, a tradition was being kept that kings of Israel received their crowns in the Temple and in close contact with the Pillar Stone set there by their forefather.

previous page
The Moot Hill at Scone, with a model of a Stone of Destiny for tourists to sit on.

above left
The Clootie Well on the Black Isle, once used in Pictish water-spirit worship, later dedicated to St Boniface in Christian times. According to local legend, you can leave your troubles behind with a piece of your clothing! But if you accidentally touch someone else's rag, you inherit all *their* troubles.

above right
The Venerable Bede

right
The Isle of Whithorn

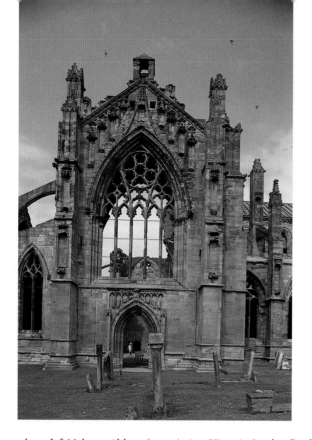

above left Melrose Abbey (permission Historic Scotland) *above right* Castle Urquhart: King Bride's stronghold was probably built on the knoll on the right (permission Historic Scotland)   *below* One of Bruce's stones lies near Clatteringshaws Loch

St.Columba

BAPTISING THEM IN THE

Stone carvings showing Eastern influence

Disaster struck Israel about 585 BC. Jeremiah had been imprisoned for prophesying bad times for his people. Then Nebuchadnezzar of Babylon beseiged Jerusalem. Two years later it fell, he destroyed the town and looted the Temple's gold. King Zedekiah escaped over his garden wall with some of his family, but Nebuchadnezzar's men caught up with him, killed his sons in front of him, put out his eyes and took him captive. There were now no male descendants of David's line left. But Nebuchadnezzar freed Jeremiah who, having rescued several items from the Temple rescued Zedekiah's daughters, one of whom was the Princess Tea, and fled to Egypt. The law of inheritance in Israel had, since the time of Moses, included the right of women to succeed to the throne. Princess Tea was of David's line, and of the blood royal. Jeremiah also rescued several items from the Temple, including the Tabernacle and the Altar of Incense, and hid them all in a cave near Pisgah. Would he have left the central item around which the Temple and his people's culture had been built—the Stone Pillar of Jacob? His scribe Baruch wrote down his next prophecy— that Nebuchadnezzar was after Egypt and its Pharaoh.

Now refugees from the eastern Mediterranean, Jeremiah, Baruch and Princess Tea disappear from biblical history.

The tribe of Dan were seafarers, whether or not they were in fact descended from Jacob's son of that name. The Greeks called sailors 'Phoenicians' (red men), for their weather-beaten skins. By about 1500 BC the Phoenicians had built a chain of ports along the Mediterranean coastline. In due course they were importing from Europe and Africa luxury goods such as ivory, gold, silver, silk, rare dyes, turning them into exports. Later their base became Carthage where they were finally extinguished by the Romans about 146 BC. They built longboats for warfare, and round ones with curved prows and sterns powered by a dozen oarsmen, for trading. These little ships ventured beyond the straits of Gibraltar, trading and setting up colonies such as Gades (Cadiz), on Spain's Atlantic seaboard. From these it was not difficult for them to trade as far as Britain and Ireland, and archaeology proves that they did so.

Jeremiah's group had to escape from Egypt. Where else could they go but to sea—and who more likely to take them than the Phoenicians, the sea-faring people, the tribe of Dan?

Phoenician trading vessels used stone as ballast.

6. Ireland

At the limit of the Phoenicians' west-coast sea routes, according to Irish tradition, an old prophet landed in Ulster accompanied by a princess, and a scribe called Simon Brech. The Chronicles of Eri called the prophet Ollamh Fodhla and say he founded a School of Prophets at Tara, and made laws based on the Ten Commandments, 'by which the nations of Eri were ruled for 1,000 years'. The Princess brought with her a harp— once the emblem of David, later the emblem of Ireland, which is said to be buried at Tara where the great stone, the *Lia Faill,* was set up.

Who were these people? Is it merely the wish to make connections that links all this in the mind? While Princess Tea, Jeremiah and Baruch were fleeing from Egypt around 580 BC, the exact date of the arrival of Ollamh Fodhla is not, at the moment, known.

Ireland is one of the most useful stepping stones in mythology because its Christianity encouraged people to develop a written script. With its long Celtic history interrupted neither by serious Roman invasion nor penetration by the English, the resulting Irish record provides a rich repository of information.

As elsewhere, the old tales would have been declaimed after triumphal battles, chanted before the inaugurations of kings, and told around firesides to circles of wrapt listeners. Only later were they written down, as four main myths, from which it is clear that the 'West', was regarded as the source of all wonders. It is taken now to mean the Iberian Peninsula— Spain. Robert Graves has connected the beginnings of the Celtic peoples with Greece, and the trail of monuments they left can be followed around the west coast of Europe. Of all the various arrivals of peoples, by far the most interesting, for the purposes of this quest, are the Tuatha De Danann— the Tribe of Dan. Like the others, they arrived on one of the main routes taken by races expanding outward from the eastern Mediterranean. They certainly came by boat—how else do you reach an island? The Phoenicians, or the tribe of Dan, were the ship-owners, and therefore not too distantly related to Jeremiah.

The Dan tribe of Irish mythology loved science, technology, poetry, art, medicine, and philosophy. They were skilled hunters, musicians and iron-workers. To the more pragmatic, this is simply the arrival of the Iron Age in Ireland, but talents like these have indeed come down through Irish and Scottish genes to the present day. These mythological Dans brought with them four treasures: the Sword of Nuada— fatal at every stroke, the fiery spear of Lugh— perpetually dripping blood, the inexhaustible Cauldron of Dagda, and the Stone of Destiny. The first Dan king of Ireland, Nuada, lost a hand in battle with a tribe of immigrants called the

Fomors (probably Belgians). Kings had to be perfectly whole so, in a magnificent gesture of reconcilitaion, he abdicated in favour of Bress, son of the Fomorian king. The name 'Bress' is of interest to us because it is not unlike 'Brec' or 'Baruch.'

The Tuatha De Danann were not the last race to arrive in Ireland. The ancestors of the Gaels arrived from Spain, led by Mile, after which there is a real mix-up between the Tuatha, the Milesians, various deities, some magic, a lot of Celtic dignity, and a few intermarriages involving Herculean tasks and lots of sex, and eventually they all settled down together. With their script they recorded genealogies, folktales, laws and sagas, creating one of the oldest literatures in Europe.

Yet none of it provides real clues to one of Ireland's most sacred places, The Hill of Tara, in County Meath. Its Gaelic title is Rath na Riogh— the Fort of Kings, and its sanctity goes far back beyond the Iron Age. All the major routes of ancient Ireland converged there. There is much excavation yet to be done, but archaeologists agree that the Hill of Tara was the seat of the High Kings of Ireland. A bank enclosed a low hill from which there is an impressive view in all directions. In it stood the *Lia Fail*, the Stone of Destiny, which historian Peter Harbison describes as 'the most obviously phallic symbol of ancient Ireland, and a monument which stresses the ritual importance of the site'.

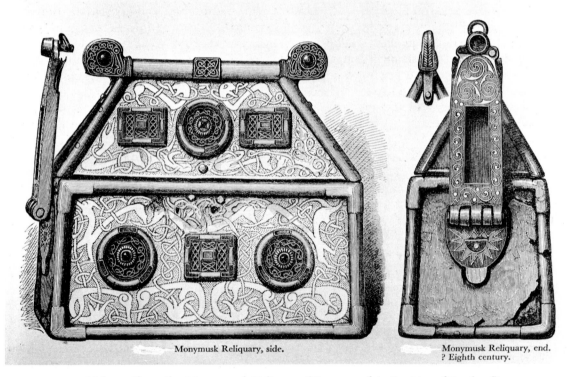

Monymusk Reliquary, side.

Monymusk Reliquary, end.
? Eighth century.

Irish motifs on the Moneymusk Reliquary (Museum of Antiquities of Scotland)

It is here that perhaps we have a link with Christianity. Harbison goes on 'In the dim shadows where mythology and history converge, Tara seems to have been in the hands of a Leinster dynasty, the Laigin. But in the early records, one can glimpse their defeat at the hands of the Ui Neill, a dynasty which was to play an extremely important role in the first 500 years of christianized Ireland.' In 1899 a fort there known as the Rath of the Synods was excavated by a group who believed it contained the Ark of the Covenant, which had been brought to Tara by the daughters of Zedekiah, one of whom was named Tea and after whom they understood the site had been named— Teamhair is the Irish for her name— mutated, through usage, to 'Tara.'

Even the English realised the importance of the indigenous culture they eventually conquered. One English antiquarian, Vallencey, saved an ancient poem, translating it for an Irish grammar book he wrote in the 18th century, to help redress 'the repeated indignities of late years cast on the history and antiquities of this once famed and learned island . . .

> Seven ladies of the chiefest quality
> Followed the fortunes of the stout Milesians
> When they resolved to conquer or to die.
> Tea, the virtuous queen of Heremon;
> Fial the confort of the brave Lughaidh;
> Fais was a princess of distinguished beauty,
> And the beloved wife of Un; and Sceine
> Was wedded to Amergin's princely bed;
> Liobhradh was the royal pride of Fuaid:
> Scota, the relict of the great Milesius,
> And Oghba, strictly chaste in widowhood.

No serious historian would dare to suggest that Zedekiah's daughter Tea could have married the Irish King Eochaid the Heremon. And yet— it is not impossible, and it would make such a good story . . .

And who was the prophet Ollam Fodhla?

According to O'Cleary's *Leabhar Gabhala* or Book Of Invasions And Conquests, he was the son of Fiacha Fionnscothaigh, and ascended the Irish throne Anno Mundi 3236 (526 BC) and remained there for forty years. He was *given* the title Ollamh Fodhla because it means 'professor', 'doctor' or 'learned man' and he was made king because of his great wisdom. He was the first king to hold the Fes, or Parliament of Tara, and the first to ordain district chiefs in Ireland. History does not record his original name. Dare we link Simon Brech with Jeremiah's scribe Baruch, connect Tara with a Judean Princess who had passed through Egypt as the guest of Pharaoh on her flight from Nebuchadnezzar— the sole survivor of David's line? Could she have been given the eponymous name 'Scota' by later writers because she wed Eochaid the Heremon, became Queen of the 'Scots' as the Irish were then known, and mother to a royal Irish-Scottish dynasty? Probably not— but because none of this is either provable or disprovable as yet we are free to dream.

People have been doing this for a long time. The Rev J. B. Bartnette, writing in the *Jewish Chronicle* of September 1872, was convinced Ollamh Fodhla was 'no less a personage than the prophet Jeremiah himself, who with a remnant of the tribe of Judha emigrated to Ireland at the time of the Babylonian captivity, and became the great reformer, law-giver and ruler in that famous Western Isle', and that 'he brought with him Jacob's Stone known in Ireland as *Lia Fail*, or Stone of Destiny' and that idea has not entirely disappeared.

There was a tradition that this Stone was called 'fatal' because if an impostor placed himself on it in an attempt to make himself king, it would remain silent, whereas when a prince of the blood-royal sat on it, it would cry out, giving an inafallible sign of his right to accede to the crown.

What happened to this Stone? There is one built into the parapet walk of Blarney Castle which is said to confer the gift of persuasive speech on anyone who should kiss it, and which was clearly not silenced by the birth of Christ. The official guide book actually claims that the Blarney Stone is a part of the Scottish Stone of Destiny which was given to one Brian Boru for his help in fending off an enemy. It remains as another example of a piece of rock credited with magic powers. The fact that, annually, thousands of visitors pay money to kiss it shows how much such a stone still means, however ridiculous it must seem to the wholly rational.

The use of ritual stones in Ireland is well documented by archaeologists and historians. One such is the Turoe Stone, near Bullaun in Co Galway. It is a domed granite cylinder 1.68 metres high, dating from the last few centuries BC, carved with complex and beautiful curvilinear trumpet-ends, triskeles and stylized animal heads. Harbison says there is evidence that the designs may originally have been emphasised 'in a variety of colours'. He also suggests it was used as an oracle like the Omphalos stone at Delphi.

By studying carvings like those on the Turoe Stone, anthropologists have been able to trace more accurately the sources of the Irish people, from France, Spain, Belgium and Britain, and to corroborate the information in the *Book of Inva-sions* which makes Spain look like a staging post on the Celtic route to Ireland as they came north in the wake of the Romans. The *Ora Maritima*, written by Avienus in the middle of the fourth century AD, contains elements of an early Greek voyage of exploration somewhere around the 6th century BC. He mentions the presence of Celtic tribes on the North Sea, France and Spain at that time. As the Roman occupation began to fade in Britain, trade developed across the Irish Sea and, by the end of the fifth century AD, the northern Irish, confusingly then known as the Scotti, were colonising Argyll, naming it after their own people, the Dal Riata, and bringing with them their way of cutting Ogham inscriptions on stone, the earliest surviving form of Irish writing. Did they bring a piece of the *Lia Fail* with them, or some other special Stone?

ꝺeꝂꞇ euꝺꞇꞹꞔ꞉ꞁꝺ
us ꝼꞁꞷꞁꞁꞷꞃꝺuꝺ
ꞇꝯuꝺ ꝓꞇ꞉ꞔꞁꞃ ꝼꞷꝺ

Calligrapher George Thomson's sample
from The Book of Kells

34

7. Romans and Christians

Various theories about the Stone have been formed by scholars in recent times, and these take us first of all to the period when the Romans occupied Britain, for one school of thought is that the stone used at Scone was a recycled Roman altar.

We know that the Irish *Lia Fail* remained at Tara till 1798, when it was removed to mark the burial place of some rebels—the Croppers. If it never left Ireland, from whence appeared the Scottish Stone? As we have seen, one tradition suggests that a small part of it may have been brokent off and brought to Scotland, either with the early immigration to Dalriad, or with Columba to Iona, but what other stones might have been used for the inauguration of Scottish kings at Scone?

There is plenty of evidence that the early people who dwelt in central Scotland worshipped fetish stones. Might they not have cast acquisitive eyes on magic edifices that apparently conferred wholesale success upon their Romans worshippers? The Romans carved stones for altars, distance signs and other permanent markers and left them littered around their walls, forts and marching stations. Over the six centuries between their departure and the arrival of MacAlpin one of these altar stones might well have been made into a cult object, as writer Janet B. Christie was suggesting in the 1950s.

Roman writers thought of Caledonian folk as wild barbarians, with their inter-tribal warfare and their brightly checked clothing. Julius Caesar and the historian Cornelius Tacitus both wrote about the 'Picti'—who communicated in pictures, both in their body-paint and in their stones. When Agricola was building the first line of Roman forts on the Forth-Clyde line, and reaching the vast swamp of Stirling Moss in 83 AD, Caledonians were hiding in Crannogs (large wooden islands found in inland lochs) rolling boulders from fortified hilltop duns, throwing spears at sea-faring attackers from stone-walled brochs, and squabbling among themselves. They didn't stand a chance against Roman organisation and weaponry. Agricola's son-in-law Tacitus came north to help him. Some of their Pictish prisoners leaked the information that a major attack was imminent. Much remains unclear, but it seems that a leader, named by the Romans 'Calgacus', ('Calgaich' or 'swordsman') at last persuaded his Caledonians to unite against their common predator. At the showdown (called 'Mons Graupius' by Tacitus) near Bennachie, 30,000 fearless Caledonian warriors 'tall, fair or red-haired . . . in primitive tartan . . .their shields and helmets gay with enamel . . . followed by . . . half naked, barefoot infantry' hurled themselves suicidally at the Roman army. T a c i t u s wrote 'On the succeeding day, a vast silence all around, desolate hills, the distant smoke of burning houses, and not a living soul descried by the scouts,' making out that Mons Graupius had been a great conquest. Yet Tacitus left Britain only months later, and the Romans trickled southwards till the arrival of Hadrian in 122 AD who stretched his wall from the Solway to the North Sea, marking the new limit of the Roman Empire.

Tired of constant trouble from the Caledonians, Hadrian's successor Antoninus Pius ordered another invasion. Accordingly, in 142 AD, his governor, Lollius Urbicus, marched north to strengthen the wrecked forts of his predecessor and build the Antonine Wall. It was only partially effective for about twenty years. By the end of that century the Roman Empire in Britain, weakened by a terrible epidemic, poor leadership, corruption and an over-stretching of their resources, imploded. The joyous Caledonians quickly repossessed their territory.

Gloom shrouds the ensuing Dark Ages, but we know that, while late in the 4th century Saxons were attacking the south east coast of Caledonia, the west was being raided by fierce Irish warriors seeking slaves —*Scotti* means 'raiders'.

Did the Caledonians help themselves to artefacts from derelict Roman habitations? Modern history demonstrates that it is normal for people to save the souvenirs of their occupation, so it is possible. That the Romans used places of worship along the Antonine Wall is without doubt, though. Several altars have been found and can be seen in the Hunterian Museum of Glasgow University. Christie made a study of these, suggesting that they resembled seats or chairs. Certainly any verbal description of them—the depression in the surface, the volutes at each side—could be said to match descriptions of the Stone. Christie's favourite was found in 1771 at Castlecary to the east of the A80 near Falkirk, cut from local limestone, 15 inches high, its top 15 inches by 11 inches with volutes at each side 3 inches in diameter. In the centre is a round basin

7 inches in diameter and five-eighths of an inch deep. What's left of the pediment bears an inscription—'DEAE'. Persuasively, Christie argues that the complete altar could have been two to three feet high, and the completed Latin inscription could have meant something useful. In fact the proportion of most Roman altars is pedestal-like, tall and narrow—and there is no reason to believe this one would have been different when complete. Anyone sitting on top would look as though they were perched on an ornate bird-bath or an elevated stone commode, their feet dangling several inches above the ground.

Dr Lawrence Keppie, Senior Curator of Archaeology and History at the Hunterian, is 'not aware of any examples of altars or parts of them being carried away to Pictish or Scottish sites', though 'Certainly stonework was removed for re-use . . . for example at Jedburgh Abbey'.

Dr Keppie also suggests we consider the mysterious Black Stone which has been in the University of Glasgow since its foundation in 1451. This is on view, set in an 18th century chair. There were once similar stones at Edinburgh and Aberdeen, and one remains at St Andrews. 'I imagine these stones fall within a general category of ceremonial seats of which the Stone of Destiny is a conspicuous example'. Perhaps, all along, the Stone has been on public view!

There is one tenous trail of tradition that links the Stone of Destiny with the little towns of Whithorn and Melrose in the south of Scotland. Whithorn lies three miles from the end of a headland jutting southward into the Solway Firth, and has clearly been perceived to be a particularly holy place for a very long time. Local place-names reverberate with ancient sounds— the Mote of Druchtag, the Doon of May, the

opposite Remains of the Antonine Wall at Bearsden; *right* The Black Stone, built into a chair in the 18th century, on view at the Hunterian Museum, Glasgow

Standing Stones of Drumtrodden, and St Ninian's Cave. The peninsular tip, the 'Isle' of Whithorn, has always embraced a harbourful of ships, being on one of the earliest sea routes, and there is a little ruined chapel at which visiting pilgrims used to land.

Constantine the Great had declared Christianity the official state religion of the Roman Empire in the 4th century and travelling evangelistic monks went preaching it. Bede (673-735), who finished his *Ecclesiastical History of the English Nation* in 731 AD, wrote 'these southern Picts . . . received the faith of truth, when the word was preached to them by Nynia, a most reverend bishop and holy man of the nation of Britons, who had been regularly instructed at Rome in the faith and mystery of the truth . . . The place, which belongs to the province of the Bernicians, is called in the vernacular "At The White House," he there built a church of stone in a manner to which the Britons were not accustomed'.

Galloway was a natural stopping-place on the ancient sea-route from the Mediterranean and Spain to the Northern Isles and Norway and, as the Romans were leaving, Christian missionaries were beginning to infiltrate the area. Little is

known of Ninian, but his relics, or preserved remains, were so revered that, by 1500, all but one arm-bone had turned to dust. King James IV had it encased in silver. Someone must have rescued it from the Reformation, for it turned up in the chapel of the Scots Seminary at Douai in Belgium, where it was last seen in 1785 by Carruthers, a priest from Dumfries.

One of the earliest Christian monuments in Scotland was discovered near Whithorn. Inscribed in Latin: 'We, Latinus, 35 years, and his daughter, 4 years, praise the Lord. The grandson Barrovadus set up this memorial.' It dates from the mid-fifth century, well before Kenneth MacAlpin's time, and shows clearly that stones regarded as being special were being carved in Scotland.

Archaeologists, who have been working on the site under Dr Peter Hill since it was rediscovered in 1984, have found low walls that mark the site of a chapel which is almost 1300 years old. They have found pieces of amphorae (wine jars) from the East Mediterranean, table-ware from North Africa, French cooking vessels and fine drinking glasses, all fifth century luxury items that demonstrate the wealth and prestige that once appertained to Whithorn. Every year from April till October teams of archaeologists work on this magnificent dig, and they welcome and inform interested members of the public. The Whithorn Trust Museum shows the latest finds.

Close by the chapel, people have been burying their dead ever since its beginnings, and because of the anaerobic conditions of the soil—particularly in one part of the site—some of the remains are remarkably well preserved. Skeletons of people who, in their lifetimes, witnessed the arrival of many famous Scots, were laid bare as their graves were measured and any scraps of clothing or possessions were conserved. The very teeth that must have smiled at King Robert the Bruce were there for all to see.

Whithorn survived the Viking raids. St Ninian's Shrine became a focus for pilgrims from Europe, who regarded the journey as a spree as well as a penance. Just as in Lourdes today, places of pilgrimage drew wealth from their visitors. But Whithorn suffered bad times too, such as when the Cathedral and the town were burned to the ground in 1286.

opposite left Fifth-century memorial to Latinus; *opposite right and this page* Early carved stones at Whithorn

That Robert the Bruce visited Whithorn is historical fact. He was fifty-four and suffering a painful and life-threatening disease. In 1328 the Pope had withdrawn his excommunication, which gave Bruce some psychological relief, and he set out on his pilgrimage to St Ninian's Shrine in February 1329. He wanted to make his peace with God, and it had been near a kirk dedicated to St Ninian that he had enjoyed his great triumph at Bannockburn. After a difficult journey through the biting cold of a Scottish winter he reached Whithorn on 1 April. He spent four or five days there, praying and fasting, before making his painful way home. The Old Edinburgh Road—the pilgrims' route via Clatteringshaws Loch to Whithorn, some of which can still be walked, is marked with one of Bruce's Stones.

What does any of this tell us? That Whithorn was a much-frequented port, Christianised very early. It had strong links with all the places through which Jacob's Pillow is believed to have travelled. Stone was carved there from the earliest times. Whithorn was one of the landfalls used by travellers from Ireland to Edinburgh. Its monastery was one of a chain across lowland Scotland, which included Melrose and Lindisfarne. Whether or not an important Stone passed through Whithorn in the early days we do not know, but Whithorn, as an important religious centre, did connect with Melrose and other monasteries.

In response to a request for information circulated to newspapers throughout Scotland, a postcard arrives. Written in capitals, it reads: 'The black oblonged piece rock which came from

The skeletons of people who might have seen Robert the Bruce (Whithorn Trust Museum)

St Ninian in 803 AD is buried 12 ft below the altar in Melrose Abbey. The stone in London which is the same size is a faked'. This may well be another mixture of half-digested material, manifested by the incorrect date given for St Ninian— but this is exactly how legend grows, and therefore merits brief investigation. Very possibly it will lead down a blind alley, alternatively it might alert us to something we have not before considered.

The original monastery of *Mailros*, referred to by Bede in 731, had been founded by St Aidan a century earlier with monks brought from Iona via Lindisfarne, three miles east of the present Abbey. One of the earliest priors was Cuthbert, who lived there before taking over as prior of Lindisfarne, on which Mailros was dependent. David 1 (1124-53) found the site unsuitable and, according to the *Chronicle of Melrose* , the new Abbey was consecrated on Sunday 28 July 1146. Generations of Scottish monarchs patronised the Abbey and it became one of the richest monasteries in the kingdom. Alexander 11 had himself interred there even though he died near Oban in 1249, and Robert the Bruce was known to have an affection for it. Kings of England, notably Edward I, sacked it over and over again and Bruce kept rebuilding it. In a letter addressed to his son dated 1329 he asked him to see that the rebuilding continued, and to make sure his heart was buried there when he died.

Melrose Abbey is built from rose-coloured sandstone quarried from the nearby Eildon hills. Lofty arches still bear the most intricate carvings and traceries. Looking skyward the eye is caught and held by strange little human faces carved high in the stonework. Much of the best work was done by the Parisian stone mason John Morrow who introduces himself on his tombstone thus:

John Morow sum tyme callit was I and born
in Parysse certainly and had in kepyng all

mason werk of Santandroys ye hye kyrk ofglasgw melros and paslay of nyddysdayll and of galway I pray to God and Mari baith and swete Sanct Johne to kepe this haly kirk fra skathe

Morrow is claimed as the first Master of the Freemason Lodge at Melrose, one of the oldest in Scotland.

The ruined skeleton of the Abbey now springs from trim gardens where the old monastery walls are bedecked with climbing roses in red, gold and white, entwined with purple clematis. On a sunny day in summer it basks in the appreciation of busloads of tourists, but there is a darker side to Melrose too, as a succession of its custodians will testify.

Jimmie Blain has been Custodian of Melrose Abbey for twelve years. Local people ask Jimmie if he has been visited by the White Lady yet. So far she seems to have given him a wide berth, but he tells of areas within the oldest parts of the Abbey where, when he or one of his workers is raking the gravel, a different sound is wont to echo beneath their feet. He wonders what archaeologists will find, when eventually these hollow depths are dug. One evening recently, after the crowds had gone and just before closing time, a family group arrived, with their dog on its leash. Jimmie accompanied them, chatting about the Abbey's past, their feet crunching on the gravel. Just inside the west entrance of the Nave—where the hollow sound is heard—the dog stopped, its hackles rising. It stood rooted to the ground shivering and whimpering with fear. What is it that lies beneath—and could it include the old Stone of Destiny?

The Abbey undoubtedly houses the mortal remains, and possibly therefore the shades, of some remarkable individuals. At the time when the 1888 guidebook was written by Mr J. Wass, the custodian of that time, the heart of Robert the Bruce was still believed to lie buried beneath the

High Altar in the Chancel at the easternmost end of the Abbey. But then so are the mortal remains of Michael Scott, the wizard credited with separating the nearby Eildon Hills into three.

A recent letter from George Smith, retired custodian, states:

> About the black stone under the High Altar, there is no specific mention of it in any books or charters. However it is my belief that after the destruction of the Abbey in 1385 when the much revered black marble Holy Rood was broken, a piece of it was saved and buried under the High Altar when the Abbey was being rebuilt.

The Black Rood of St Margaret, in its gilded silver case, was looted from Edinburgh Castle by Edward I along with the Stone of Scone in 1296, but unlike the Stone, it was returned. David II (1329-71) lost it at the Battle of Nevill's Cross, but it later found its way to Durham Cathedral, disappearing from there at the Reformation. But would such a venerated relic really have disappeared?

Perhaps something of interest does indeed still lie hidden beneath the altar. Some years ago there was an excavation there. A mummified heart was found in a leaden casket. Although at that time it could not be positively identified it was re-interred 'somewhere' in the garden of the abbey. Perhaps at some date in the future it will be matched through its DNA with the skeleton presently resting in Dunfermline Abbey.

No Stone of Destiny has so far been found at Melrose. And yet there are odd connections with other traditions: a stone shield is carved on one of the walls, showing the rebus of a mell or mason's mallet and a rose. George Smith reminds us that 'The Knights Templar have a stone in their keeping, which they claim is the original one'. And Melrose has links with the Knights Templar, as we shall see later. What connection has Melrose with Whithorn? There was one individual in whom there was invested a reverence for Whithorn, a love of Melrose, the wealth and the motivation to help in the preservation of both places, some connection with the Knights Templar, and secret knowledge of the whereabouts of the Stone of Destiny, and that person is none other than Robert the Bruce himself.

The Stone of Destiny, then, may have been a Roman Altar, though perhaps this is unlikely. It could have been brought in to Scotland via Whithorn as a holy object, along with the earliest Christians. But something is hidden at Melrose.

Stone carvings at Melrose Abbey

8. Dalriada and the Royal Boar

If the Stone of Destiny came in to Scotland from Ireland, one of the most likely routes was via the lochs and waterways of the ancient kingdom of Dalriada— now western Argyll—and a fort there, whose name crops up in the legends, is Dunadd.

Marion Campbell, whose family roots reach far back towards the earliest times in the area, writes lovingly of the low-lying lands between Lochgilphead and Crinan. For her the very name *A'Mhoine Mhor* (the Big Moss) 'has the sough of winds in it'. Near the north-eastern end of *A'Mhoine Mhor* Dunadd rises less than two hundred feet, where 'it crouches like a great lion'. The causeway leading to it is now a farm track 'down which have gone the feet of spearmen, riding-ponies, pack-horses and royal chariots, for it was once the high road to a capital.' Nowadays one will always encounter one or two people, for it draws both the curious passer-by and the expert.

The river Add wanders westward from its source in Loch *Sitheanach* (loch of the fairy mound) high in the hills between Loch Awe and Loch Fyne, coiling lazily round the foot of the rock in shiny black curves, meandering on to Loch Crinan, a slip of silver in the distance. Campbell writes:

> The tide itself once washed where now the mist lies, at the lip of a shelf carved by cold seas out of glacial drift, in that long age when

land and sea played a slow see-saw and the rocks escaped from their vast ice-coffin. That was before the hunters came northwards from the lands where their far ancestors had caught Rhone salmon or chased the wild bulls of Altamira. When the first man trod this ground is still an unanswered question; perhaps he came towing a sledge and hooded in deerskin to fish among the floes where the fat shoals swam; perhaps he traversed bleak tundra from pocket to stunted pocket of scrub-willow; perhaps already he braved the open sea . . . When the ice-fed sea was highest it made a bay of Crinan Moss and an inlet of Glassary Glen . . .

Archaeologist Ronald Morris agrees with Campbell that until somewhere between 2,000 and 1,500 BC, the sea was higher than it is now, 'perhaps by about 25 ft', which helps us to date the earliest of the carvings, and to tell us that the people who made them came by sea and were 'perhaps among the very first inhabitants when our Scottish land became really inhabitable after the last ice age ended'.

A local tradition claims that ships once berthed at the base of the rock. Backing up this legend, the shattered remains of red Samian ware, pottery the Romans used, and of Gaulish wine jars, have been found. Adamnan wrote of the French wine ships coming 'to the head of the region'.

As boat expert and Greenwich scholar Patrick Carnie explains, the curraghs plying between Ireland and Scotland, sturdy skin-covered boats, were well capable of carrying the Stone of Destiny. Like the Phoenicians, they used boulders as ballast.

In the years between 500 and 800 AD Dunadd was head of its region, Dalriada. Celtic tribes often fortified a hill central to their territory for their capital, and inaugurated their kings there. Campbell takes us up the steep climb from the causeway, through a cleft in the rock a hundred feet above the plain. 'Here, within a massive girdling wall, is a green level strewn with hut-ruins and a well whose spring now supplies the farm below. A grass-grown stairway leads to higher terraces, the topmost of them still bearing part of a curved citadel-wall, and below it to the northward a bare sheet of rock.' This outcrop bears six worn carvings; a deep cup surrounded by a faint ring, an excised line-drawing of a boar, and two footprints, one clearly defined size 8

and another, more shadowy. There is also Ogham writing. The Dal Riata used this simple form of writing, slash marks starting from a single line, and at Dunadd it can be seen in the shadows produced by low sun.

After sitting quietly in its Moss for a thousand years, Dunadd returned to the attention of the public through the researches of Skene in 1850. Victorian archaeologists' clumsy excavations destroyed stratification—the layers which denote different periods of occupancy—and they were inclined to take home, then lose, artefacts. The Society of Antiquaries of Scotland carried out digs there in 1904-5 and 1929, but learned little from the exercise. Most of what we do know of the early days at Dunadd comes from Irish writings. Even the earliest Irish annals were written long after the events they refer to, dating from around 563 to about 740 AD, but the source was the oral tradition that was passed down from generation to generation in the way we have seen earlier, in this case telling of the people of

The Boar carving pictured in 1965 before capping

The hillfort Dunadd, Argyll

a small kingdom on the coast of County Antrim who, by the fifth century, were migrating to the seaboard of Argyll. They had a leader called Reuda, or Riata. Fergus son of Erc, a contemporary of St Patrick, ruled the Dal Riata people in Ireland, and is believed to have established authority over this area of Argyll. He died in 501 AD having started a dynasty that would expand Dalriada to the borders of the British kingdom of Dumbarton on the shores of the river Clyde, and eventually to the Pictish kingdoms of the north

and east. The descendants of his grandsons Comgall—who gave his name to the Cowal peninsula—and Gabran were known of in the eighth century.

Whoever founded Dalriada, by the eighth century their descendants had fortified duns at Dunaverty, Tarbert, and Dunollie as well. There were years of uncertainty, Dunadd was beseiged in both 683 and 736— but eventually a new name appears from the descendants of Dalriadic kings, that of Kenneth Mac Alpine,who is

45

believed to have had quite a bit to do with the Stone of Destiny.

Of the practice of rock-carvings, Morris writes, 'over three thousand five hundred years ago, an unknown race of men began, for the first time in the British Isles, to carve on stone.' These early carvings of hollows, squiggles, circles and spirals known as 'cups and rings' still puzzle archaeologists. In Argyll alone there are about eighty sites, forty seven of which are near Dunadd. There are certain constants in these carvings. They are found on moveable slabs and often occur on 'the living rock'—part of the underlying geological structure. Carvings on outcrop rock are usually 'within 20 degrees of horizontal' and are set where there is an open view of a waterway. Most are also within walking distance—six miles—of places where gold or copper ore was extracted in early times. All of these conditions are fulfilled at Dunadd, where jewellers and fine metalworkers plied their trade.

At present, archeologists beleive rock carvings had ritualistic significance, to do with the sun, for ceremonies such as burial, for practical purposes to do astronomy and metal prospecting, and for the inauguration of kings. The practice of placing of a new king's foot or feet in specially carved-out 'footprints' has been discussed in Chapter 1. One can envisage the rising sun illuminating the new king after his night-long vigil, the cup full of oil, or blood, for sacrifice or for anointing him. Campbell notes that the footprints are 'so placed that anyone who stands in them faces the distant crests of Cruachan . . . fourteen hill-forts stand within sight of Dunadd . . . it is possible that from their walls the shields flashed in salute and the hilltop fires blazed out on coronation night'.

The Dal Riata of Dunadd organised their society according to principles of law which were to become fundamental in Scotland. Campbell explains:

Celtic kings were probably, like any other primitive king, half-divine; on their courage and integrity depended the health of the people and the fruitfulness of the land; but they were not absolute monarchs. They remained subject to the law (as indeed the Crown in Scotland is still under the laws and can be sued through its ministers), and the law was in the hands of a class of highly-trained jurists, the *Breitheamhan*, men of the priestly caste which stood above the warrior-caste from which the kings were drawn.

The footprint at Dunadd in 1965 before capping

To reach this rank you had to pass through a strenuous training, in which nothing was written. Everything had to be committed to memory. If you passed through all three of the mysterious seven year-long training periods you became what the Roman writers called a druid.

It is thanks to St Patrick that any fragments of the law were written down, though he selected only those laws that did not conflict with Christianity. These still pertained in medieval Scotland. Contract is the fundamental principle, whether between God and man, king and people, or man and woman. Intention of offence is healed by appropriate compensation. Failure to make good a breach of contract resulted in outlawry, the worst punishment, because the individual banned from the group is without protection. A king inaugurated on Dunadd was entering into a contract with his people, and a contract with God.

The Dunadd Ogham, though Irish in type, has not yet proved translatable, which makes it more like the enigmatic Oghams of the Picts. The boar carving, too, is a Pictish symbol, while lacking certain features that would make this attribution definite. These two pieces of evidence suggest some Pictish connection with Dunadd. The Picts communicated through a whole vocabulary of animals, birds, fish and serpents as well as strange symbols. Professor Duncan suggests that some of these symbols represent objects used in the 1st century, and that they were depicted on perishable materials or in tattooing till the period in which they appear on stone. The carvings are believed to denote the identity of great warriors or leaders, each symbolised by a particular animal deity with whom the ancestor of the person commemorated is associated. Who was symbolised by a boar? Possibly Angus 1, an early king of Picts who either conquered the Dal Riata or merged with them. Is it not likely that the ancestral symbol of a Pictish king would be carved on any Stone used at his inauguration too?

At Dunadd, therefore, there is clear connection with Ireland, with Irish kings, their king-making ceremonies and religions. The sea-route to Ireland had been used since the earliest times. The Dal Riata were highly artistic and skilled. They made rock carvings, and used existing ones. The summit rock shows workmanship of periods spanning 2,000 years. Are the Dal Riata likely to have left behind in Ireland their special Stone—one reputedly been blessed by St Patrick himself? Is it not possible that they would have brought at least a part of it with them? And, in a society for whom art and carving on rock were normal means of communication, and part of their king-making ceremonies, it would at least appear likely that a venerated object such as the Stone of Destiny would be richly decorated.

Ogam writing at Dunadd which has never been deciphered

9. Columba, King of Storms

Some of the legends about the Stone of Destiny say that it was St Columba's pillow, some that it was his altar, others connect it with the Hebridean island of Iona in some way. Perhaps we should look at how Columba would have used such a stone, in order to weigh up the evidence for any of these theories.

Many people have written about Columba. The first to do so was Cuimine the Fair, Abbott of Iona just sixty years after Columba's death. Later Adamnan quarried Cuimine's work for his own 'life' of the saint.

Peering through the hagiographic mists, in which Adamnan 'proves' how the saint's life was predestined in the bible, we search almost in vain for Columba the individual. His birth is heralded by an angel which appears to Eithne, his mother, in a dream and presents her with an exquisite cloak glowing with the colours of all the flowers in creation. She is to bear a son of great beauty—

A youth shall be born out of the north
With the rising of the nations;
Ireland shall be made fruitful by the great
flame,
And Alba, friendly to him.'

Thus he will be remembered throughout history. This gives us a clue to medieval thinking. These early Christian evangelists liked to emulate the behaviour of their Biblical predecessors, and those who wrote about them later liked to confirm their likeness to Really Holy People by showing that they lived in the same way. Accordingly, Columba's birth is announced like the birth of Christ, and he later has a Jacob-type dream on the pillow-stone which was later set up to mark his grave. Columba may in fact have slept on stone, genuinely to follow his hero Jacob, and here Adamnan may well have been documenting fact. He had at his disposal both written and oral sources. People living at the time of Columba were also accustomed to seeing stone and wood and metal that had been carved into intricate and beautiful designs, first pagan then with Christian symbols added, and we can take it that he was familiar with such art.

Columba was born in Gartan, Donegal, it is said on Thursday 7th December 521 AD, and his life must indeed date from about that year. His clan, the royal Ui Neill mentioned earlier in the chapter about Ireland, ruled the north of Ireland from Tara and Armagh, both ancient centres of Druid activity. Art historian Ian Finlay writes of the ritual stone heads which can still be seen in Armagh cathedral, and at Tara, of 'the Stone of Fal, a phallic monument which vented a shriek in the presence of a rightful king' which, as we have seen, remained there till the eighteenth century. Columba, then, grew up among carved and magic stones. Yet although eligible, Columba

Torr Abb

was not groomed for kingship. Instead he was given in fosterage to Cruithnechan, a priest, and baptised with the name of the dove, for peace, perhaps as a family offering to the church. The practice of sending a child into fosterage was normal at that time, and the resulting relationships were as close as blood-ties. He studied under some of the greatest teachers of his day, and he was what we might today call especially gifted. After his ordination, he spent fifteen years preaching around Ireland and founding monasteries like Durrow.

In spite of his peaceful name, Columba was clearly a stirring fellow. Tradition says he did something to cause the terrible battle of Cooldrevne (561) in which many Irishmen were killed and that, for this sin, he was excommunicated. Either St Molaisi intervened, imposing on him instead the penance of perpetual exile from his native country, or he imposed the exile on himself. Why? Finlay writes 'One grasps at straws as pointers to the truth, and the only wisp is the celebrated *Cathach*.' The *Cathach* is a psalter which Columba allegedly copied against the

wishes of his superiors. It still exists, in Dublin.

At any rate, some time in 563 AD, probably in early summer, Columba set off across the sea, with twelve companions. After a journey of 100 miles, his boat grounded on a steep pebble beach at the south end of the island known then as I or Y, now as Iona. The place where he landed is now called *Port a Churaich* (port of the Coracle). He then climbed to the top of the highest of the nearby hills. Ireland had disappeared below the blue line of the horizon, and he placed a stone on the spot which is still called *Carn Cul re Eirinn* (Cairn of the Back to Ireland). Whether it is true that he brought with him part of the *Lia Fail* as a parting gift from Tara, he may well have brought his own altar. We know that these travelling altars were sometimes made of stone—and also that they were occasionally imported from the Holy Land.

What did Columba find on arrival on Iona? The prospect from *Carn Cul re Eirinn* is not very promising, but as they walked northwards through the wildflowers and butterflies of the machair the island's true potential must have revealed itself.

It is an island full of magic stones. Green is its main colour, the green of sea grasses and pasture, fringed with white sands to the north, buttressed against storms raging up the Irish Sea by rocky headlands and jagged gullies at its southern end, where knobs of translucent green marble roll and tumble in the surf. Measuring only about four miles by two, its highest hill, Dun I, is less than 900 feet above sea level. Columba was probably not the first human being ever to walk this small Eden, for traces of Bronze Age life have recently been found, but he and his monks evolved a simple life there. He lived in a beehive-shaped cell built of smooth stones from the shore covered with a wooden framework and a turf roof, which he called 'my little hut', and which was situated 'on the higher ground', believed to have been the rocky mound of Tor Abb, on which evidence of early building has been found. He and his faithful attendant Diormit were on good terms. There was a bell which he could ring to summon the other monks, and they sang prayers in their little church. They wore sandals and, for special festivals, white robes. Sometimes Columba would write in his cell, sometimes he would go on retreat to another island he called Hinba. This may have been *Eilean-na-Naoimh*, the furthest west island of the Garvellachs in the Firth of Lorne, on which beehive cells still exist. Here he would fast, pray, and sing. He also travelled throughout Scotland, weaning people away from their pagan practices, which usually involved a lot of power vested in the Druids who ruled by making people fear them. Columba's religion must have seemed wonderful—downgrading personal power, preaching kindliness to your neighbour and promising a glorious after-life especially if the present one was proving difficult.

During this time Columba became closely involved in the affairs of two kings. One of these was Brude, a king in eastern Pictland—a long and dangerous journey away. Brude's stronghold sat somewhere between Loch Ness and the North Sea, either on the rocky knoll inside Castle Urquhart, or on the hillfort of *Craig Phadraig*, to the north of present-day Inverness. Perhaps Brude had heard of Columba's miraculous powers and hoped these might help him overcome the Druids.

Adamnan describes conflict from the moment Columba arrived. The Druids, led by Brude's sick old tutor Broichan, attempted to 'cause' a great storm that would prevent Columba from sailing his small boat up 'the long lake of the river Nesa.' When Columba succeeded in reaching Brude's palace he demonstrated mercy by instantly curing him with a white stone from the Ness, which he later presented to Brude to ward off death. Stone was clearly useful to Columba. Again, one day while he was crossing the Ness, he found some people 'burying an unfortunate man, who . . . was a short time before siezed as he was swimming, and bitten most severely by a monster that lived in the water'. He persuaded one of his monks to strip off and leap into the water as bait. 'The monster . . . suddenly rushed out, and, giving an awful roar, darted after him with its mouth wide open.' But Columba made the sign of the cross, commanding the monster to leave the monk and 'to return to the deep . . . At the voice of the saint, the monster was terrified, and fled more quickly than it if had been pulled back with ropes'. Brude was delighted, and convinced. He kept his stone as a souvenir, and the monster was not seen again till the camera was invented. Now Nessie is no longer fierce, and kindly sees to it that many people are gainfully employed in the Inverness area who might otherwise have had to leave the country.

left and right Effigies showing typical clothing of Medieval warriors

Iona Cathedral—St Oran's Chapel and the graves
as they were before restoration

Columba helped the second king more reluctantly. After some sort of mental struggle out on his retreat island of Hinba, during which he got badly scourged by an angel because he wanted to appoint his friend Iogenan to the kingship of Dalriada, he was forced to ordain Iogenan's brother Aidan instead—and so badly was he wounded that he carried the scar for life.

The historians get busy now. Skene writes about the inauguration of Aidan:

St Columba had obtained at the Council of Dumceat the independence of Scotch Dalriada; and if ever there was an occasion on which the Stone of Destiny might be expected to play a prominent part, it was in the solemn rite by which St Columba constituted Aidan King, in obedience to a divine command declared in a vision, and accompanied by a prophecy regarding his successors. He ordains him by placing his hands upon his head, blessing him, using what Adamnan calls 'verba ordinationis;' but, throughout the whole description, there is not a single allusion to the Fatal Stone.

The Victorian historian Skene says his contemporary, Robertson's, theory 'by which he endeavoured to reconcile the non-appearance of the stone in the inauguration of the Scottish Kings of Dalriada with the legend which makes Kenneth Mac Alpin bring the stone from Argyllshire to Scone in the ninth century, was enthusiastically adopted by Dean Stanley in his *Historical Memorials of Westminster Abbey*,' but sums up the argument: 'Both Cumine and Adamnan speak of a stone at Iona which had been used by St Columba as a pillow, and on which he rested his head in his dying hours, and the first shape in which the legend of the stone of Scone meets us is as the pillow of Jacob . . . Columba had a vision of angels before his death,' just like Jacob.

The Pictish Chronicle records that Kenneth Mac-Alpin, in the seventh year of his reign, transported the relics of St Columba to a church which he built on the banks of the river Tay, and Skene suggests that the stone pillow may have been among these relics, 'Scone may have been that church, and it may have been subsequently used as the coronation stone'.

Finlay, the art historian, says of the Moneymusk Reliquary, thought to have contained the physical relics of the saint when they were later taken to Dunkeld, that at that time it had enormous importance and there was a tradition that if it be carried thrice, sunwise, around an army of Columba's people, victory would be theirs. This is evidence of a pagan idea being overlaid with Christianity.

Yet through all this speculation glimpses of Columba's character, his reactions to events, and a few facts, emerge. We know that Columba was indeed in the habit of sleeping on a flagstone with his head on another stone, whether or not in deliberate imitation of Jacob. This must have been very uncomfortable, even if they were padded with bracken, rushes or heather, yet it was probably drier than the earth itself. Mortification of the flesh may have been considered good for the soul, but a crippled Columba would not have been much use as an itinerant preacher. By no stretch of the imagination could he have had for his pillow a rock measuring the size of the chunk of sandstone that lies beneath the Coronation Chair at Westminster today, let alone something high enough for a future Scottish king

of fashion for royal burials, the local folk would lever up the ancient grave-slabs and plant the remains of their loved ones on top of whatever royal bones lay crumbling there already—so much easier than digging a new grave in the thin earth. During this century both the unfortunate 'Lost Ladye', immortalised in Helen B. Cruikshank's poem, who died on the *Sithean Mor* (Great Fairy Mound) and Marjory Kennedy-

The Stone believed to have been Columba's pillow

to sit on with dignity without running the severe risk of having at least a slipped disc.

On Iona, local people have used stones for a wide variety of purposes over the years and, ever since Columba's day, the island has been besieged by visitors who either wanted to take its stones away as souvenirs and talismans, or wanted to bury their dead beneath its stones. Kings, Lords of the Isles, and commoners all wanted to have their corpses parked there, halfway to heaven, so that their souls could hitch a ride with Columba. In fact this became a cumulative excercise, for after Iona had dropped out

Fraser, famous for collecting Songs of the Hebrides were buried there. The *Reilig Odhrain* (Oran's burial ground), is rich with potash from crematoria the world over, and is still used by the islanders.

Not so long ago, a stone turned up on Iona. Mairi MacArthur of The New Iona Press, whose book *Iona* (1990) is a collection of oral history about the island, is descended from generations of Iona crofters. Her family own Clachanach, (Stony Field) croft, next to the Abbey. Every year, her great-grandfather's plough kept striking an obstinate stone beneath the furrows of the field known as *Cladh nan Diseart* (Burial Place of the Hermit), down by the eastern shore. One day he set to, to dig up the offending item. It turned out to be a flattish stone with a little cross incised on one face. Today it is the only stone that is kept under lock and key in an iron cage in the Abbey Museum. It is labelled 'St Columba's Pillow'.

New stones are still turning up on the island. In June 1991 the grandson of the crofter who found the 'Pillow', ex-librarian at St Andrews University and father of Mairi MacArthur, rediscovered with her a stone he'd known since childhood, high on shoulder of Dun I, carved with the hoof-prints of animals. Neither of them knows, at this time, what it signified. There were other stones in and around the Abbey which have, in one way or another, disappeared. The marble altar, for instance, which was known as the Black Stone. MacArthur tells of Martin Martin, a traveller who came to Iona in 1695, who wrote of 'the Black Stone on which any oath sworn was most solemnly binding'. She reminds us that the description '*dubh*' (black) does not necessarily refer to the colour. It also means the possession of dark magic powers. Because of its perceived magic qualities—a piece of the Black Stone was said to be an antidote to disease in either man or beast—it was forever being used to cure 'the bloody flux' so many seemed to suffer from, and the translucent green serpentine rock commonly found at the bay where Columba is said to confer immunity from drowning on its owner.

Iona stones were always in demand. Every visitor to the island wanted to take home a souvenir, a talisman, a charm. Entrepreneurial local children, always short of a penny or two, took to supplying this demand, chipping bits off the Black Stone and selling them to the tourists. When the altar was gone, they naturally substituted pebbles from the beach. Thanks to the attentions of the many visitors, and the needs of the residents, Macarthur records that by the

1770s the altar had been 'reduced to fragments'.

Martin recorded a local belief in another Stone on Iona which, 'if an arm was stretched over it three times in the name of the Trinity, would grant skill in the steering of a ship'. This has gone too, as have the stone fonts that were said once to have stood between the Cathedral and the Nunnery which, 'if emptied of rainwater by a virgin, would ensure a fair wind for sailing'.

MacArthur mentions the Clachan Brath or Judgement Day Stones, three globes of white marble which were supposed to be turned sunwise in their stone basin by every passer-by. 'When the basin was finally worn through, this would herald the end of the world'—echoing the pre-Christian ritual of dedication to the sun. Although these too had gone from Iona by 1819, MacArthur suggests the triple basin just inside the Abbey may well have been their container.

From 1792 till 1840 the local schoolmaster Allan Maclean acted as official guide on the island. Well-liked and respected by both islanders and visitors, he took enormous interest in local history and could communicate in English. 'So strong was his feeling for his darling ruins that he could not speak with any patience of an Englishman having clandestinely carried off one of the figures that graced a tomb'. In 1819 a bunch of sailors was seen to vandalise one of the tombs, egged on by one of their officers for a double ration of grog.

Robert Chambers, writing in 1840 says "Here are deposited the remains of forty-eight kings . . . ending with Macbeth' and was clearly angry that the Abbey was used 'to build cottages and make enclosures, the stolen materials of which betray themselves everywhere.' He continues 'there were, at one time, three hundred and sixty stone crosses in different parts of Iona . . . the Synod of Argyle ordered sixty of them to be thrown into the sea . . . the spirit of destruction which reached this isle at the time of the Refor mation, and the degree of culpable carelessneess in protecting the ruins of the religious buildings observable since that period, have operated in wasting and carrying off nearly every relic . . . Among the most conspicuous of those remaining is . . . a truly rich and elegant piece of sculpture . . . the letters composing the inscription were originally run full of melted silver . . . too great a temptation to escape the rude hands of the populace.'

The nineteenth-century folklore collector Alexander Carmichael found a *leag gruagach* or milk stone, known locally as the *Clach a'Bhainne*, still in use, a few yards from the site of today's telephone boxes. The girls were in the habit of pouring a little milk over this flat stone on their way home from milking the cows out in the pasture, to placate the *gruagach*—the spirit which guarded the cattle, though most of these magic stone rituals would have developed long after Columba's day.

In order to assess the feelings Columba engendered in his people and the reverence with which his possessions were therefore regarded, we will follow him to his grave. He had based himself on Iona for thirty-four years. Adamnan writes: 'The old man, worn out with age, went in a cart one day in the month of May . . . to visit some of the brethren who were at work . . . on the western side of the island' There he told his monks he would be quite glad to die, but didn't want to cause them sorrow at such a happy time of year, so would wait awhile. 'Then . . . he turned his face to the east, still seated as he was in his chariot, and blessed the island with its inhabitants'.

Later that year, at harvest-time, the angel of death comes calling for him. He blesses the corn and says he's glad the people will have enough to eat that winter. On his way back to the monastery 'bowed down with old age' he stopped to rest. 'Behold, there came up to him a white pack-horse, the same that used, as a willing servant, to carry the milk-vessels from the cowshed to the monastery. It came up to the saint and, strange to say, laid its head on his bosom . . . and, knowing that its master was soon about to leave it, and that it would see him no more— began to utter plaintive cries, and like a human being, to shed copious tears'. Columba comforted the horse, and blessed it. After attending a service, he 'returned to his chamber, and spent the remainder of the night on his bed, where he had a bare flag for his couch, and for his pillow a stone, which stands to this day as a kind of monument beside his grave. . . As soon as the bell tolled midnight, he rose hastily, and went to the church; and running more quickly that the rest, he entered it alone, and knelt down in prayer beside the altar'. Diormit, following him, 'found the saint lying before the altar; and raising him up a little, he sat down beside him and laid his holy head on his bosom. Meanwhile the rest of the monks ran in hastily . . . and beholding their dying father, burst into lamentations . . . Diormit then raised the holy right hand of the saint, that he might bless his assembled monks. And the venerable father himself moved his hand at the same time, as well as he was able— that as he could not in words, while his soul was departing, he might at least, by the motion of his hand, be seen to bless his brethren. And having given them his holy benediction in this way, he immediately breathed his last . . . '

And so we leave Columba, the man who poet Kenneth Macleod called 'King of Storms' for his alleged ability to quell the raging sea.

It is some time later that we begin to hear about relics, altar stones and the like. A cross was still in existence, in Adamnan's day, where the old horse had made its farewell. Recently the carefully buried skeleton of a horse was discovered near the Abbey. It is at present being examined in Edinburgh. Various aspects of the

Looking eastward from Torr Abb over the Road of the Dead

burial make it look likely that it dates from the sixth century, when nobody would have bothered to inter a horse unless there was something very special about it. If we can still admit to such a fascination with everything to do with Columba, then surely we can more easily understand those earlier Scots who treasured his relics.

Iona attracts some 200,000 people from all over the world every year. Why do they come? What is it they hope to find? The answer is probably a mixture of things. While many come because of the work of the Iona Community begun earlier this century by the late Lord Macleod of Fuinary in his attempt to rediscover the simplicity of Columba's religion, others come to find peace of mind, for their own religious experience. Some come for souvenirs, photographs, or to be in a beautiful wild 'natural' environment—but most come because St Columba dwelt there 1400 years ago.

If, as seems perfectly possible, any stones connected with Columba lie undetected still, beneath the Ionian sod, or under the green waves of its sea, it is perhaps as well. For some reason we have a greed for the material relics of religions in which we no longer believe, as though they will bring us some solace. Is this perhaps why we feel as we do about the Stone of Destiny? Why the individuals who were involved in the Westminster episode of the fifties proudly sport the fragments of that Stone they were given as mementoes of that event?

10. Dunstaffnage

Iona fell victim to the Viking scourge that arose in the eighth century, its monastery sacked and its monks horribly murdered, and Columba's relics were brought to the mainland for safe keeping at Dunstaffnage, near Oban. The connection of Dunstaffnage with the Stone of Destiny is confused but persistent, for there are two periods when the Stone may have been there, and two possible keeping-places. There are those who believe it never left.

Dunstaffnage Castle squats on a knob of old red conglomerate which once boiled up from flat rocks between the Firth of Lorn and Loch Etive, Argyll. Eastward from the wall-walk, beyond the grey awkwardness of Connel Bridge, Loch Etive stretches to the foot of Ben Cruachan. Northwards lie Lismore and Morvern, and westward squats the great bulk of Mull. Much remains of the original stronghold, built for the MacDougalls of Lorne in the 13th century, who entered it through a natural rock fissure. Nearby, hidden in the woods, is a ruined chapel built soon after the Castle. The 'dog tooth' decoration of its windows matches those at the Nunnery on Iona and help date it.

Robert the Bruce took Dunstaffnage from the MacDougalls of Lorne, and it belonged to Scottish royalty for some years. That Bruce knew the whereabouts of the Stone is beyond doubt. It was not his fault if, like so many valuable hoards hidden in times of danger, it was later lost.

Writer Lorn Macintyre, who grew up nearby, wonders why Bruce, who normally demolished castles, spared Dunstaffnage. Bruce destroyed castles when the English were using them to oppress Scots. Sooner or later Edward I, realising the Stone he had stolen was a fake, would batter his way back to Scone for the real one. If it had been safe in Dunstaffnage before, why not again? And if you want to hide a large stone, what better than to build it into your nine-feet-thick wall along with hundreds more like it?

In 1470 the castle was handed over to Colin, 1st Earl of Argyll, and its custody vested in his cousin, the Captain of Dunstaffnage. Today the 22nd hereditary Captain, Michael Campbell, keeps his title by sleeping in the castle annually, on midsummer's night, and some in his family believe the Stone of Destiny is still hidden there.

Many historians down the years have taken in intense interest in the area around Dunstaffnage. Its very name rewards scrutiny, 'Dun' being Celtic for 'hill-fortress' and thus an old word, 'Staffnage' being a corruption of the Norse 'staf-an-ness' ('promontory of the staff'), and therefore a word dating from the 8th century Viking invasions. And it has had ecclesiastical associations since Columba's day. Historians are certain the dun originally had a fully Celtic name, and that the castle may be built on the mysterious lost

A Viking boat in hiding near Portree, Skye

fortress of *Dun Monaidh*, on record as a 7th century seat of the kings of Dalriada, like Dunadd. If that is true, then the association with the Stone of Destiny is very possibly accurate.

Two Celtic missionaries are connected with the area: Irishman, Maelrubha, who towards the end of the seventh century founded a church at or near Dustaffnage, referred to in a sixteenth century document as Kilmorrie, or *Cladh Morrie* (church/burial ground of Maelrubha). It was normal to plant your preaching station close to the fortified residence of the local chief, and usual to build on the 'holy ground' of a previous church. Some say Maelrubha's was at Dunstaffnage, others prefer the 'Green Chapel' across the present Dalmally to Oban road. St Convall, or Conall, is connected with an area he called 'Evonium' by Thomas Dempster, a 17th century hagiographer, and his contemporary

David Camerarius, who also used old sources, tells us St Conall was honoured by Aidan, King of Dalriada. His chapel may have been the one on a flat-topped mound two miles south-east of Dunstaffnage, near Ardchonnel Farm. Clearly the area had strong links with the Celtic church and Ireland, as well as with royalty, and any holy relics from Iona are likely to have been brought to a holy place. The problem is—which holy place?

The translators are responsible for quite a confusion of names around the Dunstaffnage area, and therefore about the possible whereabouts of any Stone of Destiny. Boece, writing his history in Latin, used 'Evonium' as an alternative name for Dunstaffnage, and this was rendered by his translator Bellenden: 'King Ewyne biggit ane castel nocht far fra *Berigon* . . . quilk wes callit eftir Dounstaffnage.'

Three royal elections and five royal burials were recorded at Beregonium/Dunstaffnage, the first of which was before King Ewin built his stronghold. Evonium, Dunstaffnage, Beregonium, three names from the same area.

Two miles northward across the mouth of Loch Etive, antiquarian R. Angus Smith was ploutering about the shore in 1870. What he found there led him to write that Dun Sniochan, a rocky mound by the sea below Ben Lora, may have been Beregonium. The requirements are all there—a local tradition that six kings once dwelt there including Fergus and Fingal, evidence of ancient building, plus the remains of a Columban church and burial ground. Might not Columba's relics have been kept here rather than at Dunstaffnage across the bay? And if so, might there not be items yet to be discovered—perhaps even the stones on which he slept?

Alternatively, Ewen de Ergadia, reputedly a vigorous and very handsome knight, great-grandson of the mighty Somerled, might have preferred to keep them at his private residence, nearby Dunollie, along with his own inaugural Stone.

Tantalisingly, none of the accounts give an exact location for inauguration ceremonies. Bellenden writes: 'Fergus . . . wes crounit in the fatale chiar of merbil, quhilk he brocht with him . . . to stabill his realme in Albion . . . In this chiar all kingis of Scotland war ay crownit, quhil the time of King Robert Bruse:'. Where?

It was in the writings of a sixteenth century character, John Monipennie, that we first come across mention of 'The most ancient castle of Dunstaffnage, in which were the kings of Scotland in old times crowned, where also the Marble fatall Chayre remayned more then one thousand yaeres'.

Late in the eighteenth century two tourists separately visited Dunstaffnage. One was told nothing about the Stone of Destiny, the other

A stone built into the wall of Dunstaffnage Castle

was given the full story. On 6th June 1760, Bishop Pococke heard the history of the castle minus any mention of the Stone, while twelve years later as we saw in the introduction, Thomas Pennant was being regaled with tales about the marble chair. Perhaps Pennant's informant was the 14th Captain Donald Campbell, or someone else who knew of a local tradition, or who had access to some lost source of knowledge, while Pococke's host simply had not heard of it.

Nigel Tranter sews up the gaping seams of known history in his attempt to understand *why* the people of the past behaved as they did. In *Kenneth*, a novel about MacAlpin, the young

The western seas, from Dunollie Castle, Oban

man, long before he is King, explores Dunstaffnage with the beautiful Princess Eithne. Lighting torches of bog pine, they investigate an underground earth-house. There they find the Stone, 'almost black, with its hollows and carvings picked out in the light of the flickering flames . . . smooth, almost like marble.' As they leave, Eithne hears a strange rushing sound. It is the giant waterfall under the sea, written about by Ossian in 'Songs of Deirdre and the Sons of Uisneach', known as the Falls of Lora. One tradition says the Stone is hidden near a great waterfall, and the Falls of Lora must be one of the most powerful in Scotland, with the entire weight of Loch Etive behind it. Tranter has MacAlpin taking the Stone to Iona, before returning it to Dunstaffnage, and going on to Dunadd to confirm his kingship while Eithne gives birth to their son.

Whether Dunstaffnage, Dun Sniochan, Dunollie, or somewhere yet undiscovered were in fact once the lost city of Beregonium, the long local tradition that the Stone lies somewhere near Dunstaffnage is worth considering.

above Loch Fyne, on the route from Dunadd to Perthshire   *below* The Pass of Brander

opposite: clockwise from top right

Loch Tay and Ben Lawyers

The Tay at Dunkeld

The Drystane House, Auchindrain Museum

The ruin of Turnberry Castle, where Bruce was born

this page: above left
Bruce at Bannockburn

above right The Wallace Monument near Stirling marks the beginning of the Highland Line (courtesy of Historic Scotland)

right Bruce died at Cardross on the River Clyde

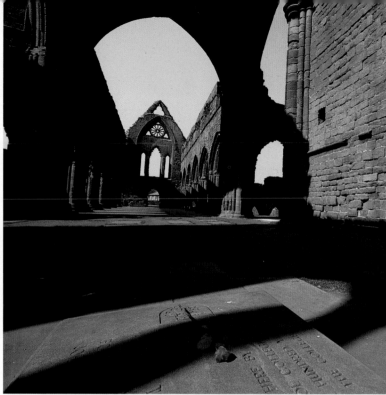

above left Lochmaben Castle, near Lockerbie *above right* Sweetheart Abbey was one of several built by Balliol's devout mother
below Dumbarton Rock

PART III

11. Scotland United

Whichever of the legends about the origins of the Stone bears the truth, by the ninth century it had arrived at Scone in what is now Perthshire.

Professor Duncan lists the peoples living north of Hadrian's Wall at that time: the Scotti in the west, Picts— believed to have been the aboriginal race—in the north, middle and east, Britons to the south. Round the coastline Vikings raped and pillaged, plundering rich pickings of meat, gold and jewels everywhere, especially from monasteries attacking Iona three times between 795 and 806 AD. The Book of Kells probably survived only because you couldn't melt it down and it had no intrinsic value. Not till much later did the Norse come to settle and bring new skills to northern Britain—Alba.

While Scots wrote Ogham, Picts communicated in comic-strip, their earliest stones depicting animals, birds and fish along with strange symbols such as Z rods, crescents and circles, later stones showing the Christian cross plus the symbols, till finally they used complete biblical iconography to show stories such as that of Daniel and the lions. It is now thought that some Pictish designs were done in colour, and this is likely, in view of their proven artistry and their noted love of brightly dyed clothing.

However all was not peace and beauty. The peoples of Alba were a pretty aggressive lot. As the population increased, groups began to amalgamate, for both defence and co-operative acts of predation. Since about 600 AD they had probably been governed by a main king, with under-kings in certain areas. Constantine (789-820), listed in the Duan of Alban—the oldest known royal genealogy of Scotland—was the last king of Picts. It was his brother Angus who is thought to have been the inspiration behind the Boar carving at Dunadd. Kenneth MacAlpin became King of the Scots in Dalriada about 839, when old Alpin his father was killed in battle. He had a Pictish name—Cinead, and a Scottish granny descended from Fergus of Dalriada— and he somehow managed to become King of everyone in Alba by about 847 AD, whether by inheritance or trickery we cannot yet tell. The story goes that MacAlpin invited all the Pictish leaders to come to a great banquet at Scone. The wine flowed freely and a great ceilidh was going on, with singing and dancing to take their minds off their troubles. Suddenly the benches gave way. They were tumbled into a great pit, and every one of them beheaded. An undemocratic, if effective, way to gain leadership.

MacAlpin's era was one of violence and change throughout Europe. He lived less than a century after Charlemagne. The Danes had just sacked London and were wreaking havoc throughout England, which wasn't unified for another fifty years. He is the first important figure of Scottish

It is thought that Sueno's stone may have been put up to show in picture form that the Picts had been conquered by Kenneth MacAlpin

history about whom a reasonable amount is known. He did move his centre of administration and his capital from Dunadd in Dalriada (Argyll) to Perthshire, though we can only speculate on his reasons for so doing. Perhaps it was in order to govern his enlarged kingdom as was Irish/ Scottish custom, from its geographical centre; maybe he wanted to be tactful—for Scone had been the sacred centre of Pictland.

Constantine had erected the Culdees' wattle church of nearby Dunkeld into a monastery, normal procedure when a conquering king wanted to confirm and sanctify his power over an area. At the point where legend begins to merge with history, around the mid-ninth century, MacAlpin had the remains of St Columba transported in the Moneymusk Reliquary to Dunkeld. In placing such a venerated Scots symbol in a Pictish shrine, he showed psychological insight. Scots were now firmly planted, both symbolically and physically, in the seat of government, and their most important symbol was a Stone of inauguration.

The Moneymusk Reliquary is a small container, yet it was afterward regarded in its own right as a sacred object, having its own dewar (caretaker). It was carried before the Scottish army at Bannockburn as a talisman, and it can still be seen in Edinburgh, where it is carefully preserved in the National Museum of Scotland. While the Monymusk Reliquiary would not have been difficult to transport overland in the mid-ninth century, the Stone of Destiny must have been a much trickier proposition. Heavy objects can be slung on poles, can be transported over bog, sod and rock on sleds. Boats and rafts can be pulled up lochs and rivers. But moving the Stone of Destiny could not have been an easy task, given the topography of Alba. Travellers then would have had to follow the same lochs, rivers and passes as the main road system does today, only instead of denuded hillsides and the

Kilchurn Castle, Loch Awe

hazards of tour buses, they would have faced bears, boars and wolves, undrained swamp and stands of virgin forest.

Somehow the procession wound its way along the shores of Loch Etive, up the River Awe through the Pass of Brander into the dark deeps beneath Cruachan, along the northern shores, past the headland on which Kilchurn Castle now stands, to Dalmally. From Dunadd the route followed the River Add, through Auchindrain to the coast at Pennymore. Then north-east via Inveraray, up Glen Aray, Glen Shira or Glen Fyne to meet the west-east paths. Onward through Glen Lochy, Crianlarich, and down the Dochart to Loch Tay. An easier passage then, below the majesty of Ben Lawers to where the black Tay pours eastward wide and strong through its strath, past Kenmore, Dull, Aberfeldy, round the wide sweep at Grandtully and southward to Dunkeld.

Tranter envisages a mile-long cavalcade, not unlike those parades of holy relics we see in Europe.

They set off from Dunstaffnage one morning in mid-April, a particularly beautiful time in Scotland, with the first greening of the country-side after winter. Even when it's raining, the air of Argyll fills with the erotic perfumes of Spring; its woodlands pink and white with anemones, the burn-sides curly with unfurling ferns, and everwhere the lushness of bluebells coming on. Through this countryside, MacAlpin's people carry their sacred Stone of Destiny towards Strathfillan and Loch Earn and then to Forteviot.

Nobles and notables greet the procession at Forteviot. There is much feasting and fun till the great day of MacAlpin's coronation, when they ride to Scone dressed in their finest clothes, accompanied by musicians. The ceremony is held in the open, by a small mound near the Church. Psalms are sung and Kenneth is elected King through a series of long speeches by the ri, the lesser kings of Alba.

He 'went to stand beside . . . the Stone of Destiny, which was now covered with the great black and white wild boar banner of Alba. When he gestured for Eithne to sit on the throne, with the children, a murmur of surprise ran through the assembly . . . He raised his hand for silence. "I, Kenneth, call upon the High Sennachie of Alba, Murdoch mac Congall, to pronounce before you all my identity and descent, that there be no mistake. Hear you him."

'An old stooping man wearing a splendid robe embroidered with the black boar . . . shuffled out from the side', to 'read' MacAlpin's genealogy but, according to ancient precedent, it is much more likely he would have sung or chanted it from memory.

After his pedigree has been pronounced pure, MacAlpin speaks. 'Now hear this. Today a great deed is to be done, and you all are witnesses to it. Under God, a new realm is to be created . . . I name it Scotia, the land of the Scots. Scotland, I say. Hear you—Scotland! . . . Only in unity will we preserve our freedom and our lands from the invaders.' He then unfurls for the first time the blue and white Saltire of St Andrew, and drapes it over the Stone of Destiny, on which he sits. The golden circlet is placed on his head by Duffus

of Fife, and everyone cheers.

In reality, MacAlpin did take charge, fighting off the Norsemen, attempting to control the Lothians in spite of its population of Angles, and drawing up the first Code of Laws for Scotland.

He ruled over the areas we now name Perthshire, Fife, Stirlingshire, Dumbartonshire, and much of Argyll. He and Eithne had a large family. Either his son or a brother, Gregor, became the founder of Clan MacGregor, which later became a threat to the unity of the Scottish throne.

Meanwhile, with the dusty remnants of a dead Columba buried under the chancel of his new stone church at Dunkeld, the Stone of Destiny planted at Scone to keep him lucky, he built himself a palace at St Andrews and a fine, timber-framed, thatched hall at Forteviot. Eithne had a house at Forfar too. MacAlpin reigned firmly and effectively over a good proportion of the Scottish people for sixteen years.

There were the fringes of course—he never quite managed to persuade either the Angles of Lothian or the Britons of Strathclyde to join him, and quelling the Vikings took even longer.

Not yet sixty, MacAlpin died at Forteviot, the ancestor of all Scottish royalty. At Forteviot today acres of fascinating lumps and bumps lie unexcavated beneath the pasture, waiting to reveal their treasures. He was buried at Iona, although it can't have been any easier getting him there than bringing the Stone east. The West of Scotland was no longer the centre of religion and government. For some reason MacAlpin was interred as 'Rex Pictorum'; not till his grandson Donald does the title 'King of Alba' appear.

By the end of the ninth century Alba was a nation. Most people were Christian. They were governed by a single King who was inaugurated upon the Stone of Destiny. But the Stone of Destiny was not the safest seat in the country. It may have conferred nationhood on the Scottish people, but it did nothing to protect the long string of kings, some good, some bad, chosen from a kind of familial short-leet for their good qualities, some mere infants, who followed MacAlpin, and whose normal form of death was murder most foul.

Dunkeld Cathedral

12. Who Owns Scotland?

With the Stone of Destiny firmly planted in Scone, in use for the inauguration of the Kings of Scotland until 1292, perhaps it is time to pause for a brief overview of some of the tortuous history of Scotland, in an effort to understand where Edward 1 of England ever got the idea that Scotland belonged to him. For it was his anger, against the people he saw as his recalcitrant vassal Scots, that caused him to wreak havoc up and down their country, and finally to wrest from them the symbol of their kingship, their Stone.

Through the centuries English kings attempted, by tricks, treaties, weddings and wars, to annexe Scotland, though the Scottish people had no such designs on the English throne. Apart from the disputed northern counties, Scots didn't covet English land either. Perhaps Edward's delusion stemmed from the very different ways in which each nation perceived the notion of kingship.

The British Isles were first governed by several small kings, the southern English beginning to unify under Aelfred the Great of Wessex around the end of the ninth century. The push northward then began. His grandson Athelstan captured York and became king of all England and, naturally Athelstan and his subjects expected the northern thrust to continue.

Meanwhile in Scotland Constantine II, inaugurated on the Stone of Destiny in 900 AD, wanted Lothian and Northumbria—good agricultural land—so much that he was prepared to do almost anything to acquire it from Athelstan. He started a trend that was to bedevil Scotland for centuries, and had to pay for his new territory by grovelling at the English king's feet.

His brother, Malcolm I, swore to be 'the English king's fellow worker both by sea and land' in return for Cumbria. In 975 Kenneth II rowed up the River Dee at Chester, with King Edgar of Wessex at the prow demonstrating his suzerainty, in return for Lothian and re-issue of Cumbria.

The practice of Scottish kings paying lip-service to the superiority of English Kings in return for border country continued. Malcolm 11 fixed the border at the River Tweed. But his successor Duncan 1 so misgoverned Scotland that the people replaced him with the Mormaer (lord) of Moray, Macbeth. Macbeth and his wife Gruoch ruled the Scots unusually well for seventeen years, persuading them into some semblance of law and order. He and his successor Lulach were the last Gaelic-speaking kings.

Peace did not last. Son of the dead Duncan, Malcolm Ceanmor grew up in England, forgot Gaelic and learned feudalism. He did not beat Macbeth and Lulach single-handed. He paid lowland and English lords for their help with land. Paying for services with good land was

Lowland landscape, scene of bloody conflicts
for land and, ultimately, for independence

repeated by later kings. But the English had not bargained for their own total defeat by the Normans in 1066. It took William the Conqueror five years to reach Scotland, where Malcolm was forced to acknowledge him as overlord of somewhere, though no one was very clear where. After Malcolm and his saintly Queen Margaret passed into history, one king after another bounced on and off the Stone of Destiny, often murdering each other for the privilege. Lowland Scotland was made feudal quite successfully thanks to kings such as David 1 (r. 1124-1153).

The feudal system was like a pyramid with God on top. He gave the King all the land of his kingdom and the Divine Right to rule it. The King leased parcels of land to his lords in return for goods and services—especially the provision of fighting men. The lords parcelled out theirs, and so on down the line. The king, being overall landowner, could re-negotiate these arrangements at will, redistributing land to peopie he liked, or to whom he owed a favour. It worked. The king commanded a centrally organised government, and had plenty of power over his nobles—they would think twice before rebelling. He had at his command an instant army without having to pay for its keep in times of peace, and he could call up local drafts whenever invasion threatened or internal troubles arose. William never actually conquered Scotland, either lowland or highland. By no stretch of the imagination did God ever donate to him any of the land north of the Tweed-Solway line.

The kinship system of Scotland was quite different. A clan chieftain's relationship with his people was supposed to be paternal, not that of a God to his supplicants. The land was common, to be grazed, farmed and roamed over more or less freely till the days of Enclosure in the eighteenth century, and the Clearances, when many clan chieftains reneged on their responsibilities. No chieftain was going to waste perfectly good fighting men on some king's military service unless he agreed with the reason.

Accident prone William (1165-1214) was called the 'Lion' because of the red lion rampant on his yellow battle flag. His horse fell on him, neatly trapping him when he tried to take Alnwick Castle in Northumbria. Delivered in chains to Henry II, he was forced to buy his freedom with homage. While Henry was having trouble with Becket, William plotted with France. Captured, he found himself in Falaise, in fetters, and this time bought his freedom by swearing away the whole of Scotland, giving the Scottish Church to the English, donating his border strongholds, lending his brother David as a hostage, and taking the bill home. In an effort to get God on his side he founded a new Abbey at Abroath— and with a spark of spirit, dedicated it to Becket.

Richard I came to the English throne full of missionary zeal, wanting cash for the Crusades. He sold Scotland back to the Scots for 10,000 silver marks—a tenth of the income of Scotland's treasury. That freedom was genuinely bought. Scots then suffered a series of child kings and

regencies. Henry III of England thought he'd found an easy number in Alexander III, crowned on the Stone of Destiny aged eight, and made him marry his daughter Margaret. She wore a robe of violet brocade with three small leopards embroidered on the front and back, and there was quite a party. Alexander duly knelt to Henry for lands he held in England but, though so young, evaded Henry's demand that he do homage and fealty for his kingdom of Scotland. Alexander said politely 'I have come hither in peace . . . to be allied to you by marriage, and not to reply to you about so difficult a question. For I have not held deliberation concerning this with my chief men, as so difficult a matter demands'.'

Historians are still divided as to whether it was tact, appeasement or duplicity that made Alexander obey a call, in 1274, to the coronation of Edward I, as his vassal. Perhaps, under these circumstances, it is not so surprising that Edward I so strongly believed that Scotland belonged to him.

Bruce put England right, briefly, at Bannockburn in 1314, and the Pope backed him up, saying he was King of Scots in his own right, and owed fealty to no-one. Yet the kings who followed Bruce went on trying to give Scotland away, pawn it, sell it. England captured David II, setting a ransom which represented three-quarters of all the taxes Scotland could raise, crippling the economy and affecting the income of every single Scot till long after his death. Plague then killed off a third of the population, leaving even fewer to pay off the ransom. 'Auld Blearie', King Robert II, crowned at Scone in March 1372, believed firmly in Scotland's independence and persuaded his Parliament somehow to pay up.

The Church next gave Scotland a rough time. Always inclined towards France and Catholicism, while Henry VIII of England was inventing divorce and espousing the Protestant cause to help him, Catholic Mary floated up the Forth to become Queen of Scots. Suddenly the people saw the light lit by John Knox. Armed with torches and Godly Truth they set out to purge Scotland of the excesses of complacent ecclesiastics, and so successful were they that when they'd finished, hardly a molecule of our historical documentation, our art, our culture, remained.

There are those who argue that the fundamentalist Presbyterianism which followed gave us our fabled work ethic, our honesty, our hunger for learning. Maybe. But it also produced a meanness of spirit, a taste for punishment, a narrow parochialism, traits not far beneath the surface of many a Scots character today, for hypocrisy lives and breathes in every glen and in every street in Scotland to this day.

The monarch who was to usher Scotland into final and binding Union with England was a woman. Queen Anne, recognised by the Scottish Parliament in June 1702, only ever visited Scotland once. She spent her seventeenth birthday in Edinburgh hating her exiled father James VII for the terrible cruelties he was perpertrating on the last of the Covenanters. Although she had eighteen children, all of whom predeceased her, and her health was so weakened by childhood smallpox and arthritis that she rushed about in a chariot like a gouty Boadicea, she did give Scotland her attention, and was personally present in the English Parliament whenever union was discussed.

It had been Malcolm Ceanmor who began the infiltration into Scotland of what has been called the 'English party', whereby Scottish lords could be bribed to promote English causes in Scotland. This process continued till Scotland finally succumbed through the Act of Union in 1707.

The disastrous Darien scheme, that misjudged attempt at colonialism, had bled Scottish coffers white, civil war was in the air, and Anne along with many others genuinely believed that union

with England was the only solution. Relations between the two countries remained poor, and England was not keen to take Scotland on board: 'Whoever married a beggar cou'd only exspect a louse for a portion', went the saying.

Scots could see the risk of being swallowed by the larger state—5,000,000 English against 1,000,000 Scots. In 1704 Scottish politicians were thinking seriously about re-establishing independence under a new monarch in spite of Anne's efforts, and they wanted nothing to do with the proposed Hanoverian succession. The

Robert Burns accused Scotland of letting herself be 'bought and sold for English gold'.

69

main reason they failed was, as ever, that they could not agree.

The English, ambitious to establish themselves as a major military power in Europe, began to apply pressure, with the Alien Act of 1705, whereby if the Scots refused to accept the Hanoverians they would be declared aliens. This meant all the property owned by Scots in England would be forfeit, and their rich trade with English colonies would be no more. On the other hand, there would be plenty of money in return for compliance. A disgusted Robert Burns accused Scotland of letting herself be 'bought and sold for English gold'.

Only a few men attended the Scottish Parliament which agreed to the Queen's commissioners being appointed to negotiate the union. Discussions only lasted from April 1706 to mid-July. In spite of 'roars of protest' when the terms were published, the Scottish Parliament voted in favour on 16th January 1707, putting themselves and their Queen out of business at the dissolution signed by her on 28th April 1707 —'ane end of ane auld song'. By the terms, theoretically, England and Scotland became one country. The two parliaments were to be dissolved and a new one created.

Scotland had 45 seats in the Commons to England's 513 and 16 peers in the Lords to 190English. While the ratio of populations was five to one (5.5 million English to just over 1 million Scots), the ratio of members was more than ten to one in the Commons, and twelve to one in theLords. There was little doubt who had the power. Soon an Act was passed which undermined the independence of the Scottish judiciary, and in 1708 the Scottish Privy Council was abolished, leaving Scotland with no effective administration.

Why had the Scots so meekly agreed to such unequal terms? Was it the act of far-seeing parliamentarians? Or of desperation? Yet, in 1713 Scots were in Parliament attempting to undo the Union. Of course they stood no chance. Fortunately the Scottish legal system, the Church, and Education were left untouched, and one positive result of the new stability was to be the Scottish Enlightenment.

In 1714 Queen Anne died, and the Hanoverians took over. There were fruitless riots. Bonnie Prince Charlie came, and went. For a hundred years Scotland got on with her own affairs until Sir Walter Scott and, through him, Queen Victoria, began to reawaken a romantic interest.

13. England's Edward and the Celtic Fringes

So much of the mystery of the Stone of Destiny depends on the actions of Edward I that it seems only fair to take a closer look at the English point of view towards the turn of the thirteenth century. It may help us to assess the persistent tradition that the original Stone has never been south of the border, and that the Westminster one was always a fake. Was Edward Plantagenet anything more than a thirteenth century thug?

At a time when kings had to be seen to be smiled upon by God—healthy, rich and powerful, the young prince Edward grew up looking like everyone's idea of a medieval hero. Born in the year 1239, he grew to an immensely strong six foot two inches in height. He could leap fully armed into the saddle without stirrups, and he was a bonny fighter.

He managed to overthrow his father's imprisoner Simon de Montfort and in 1272 he was crowned King of England. He was thirty five, full of new ideas, and deeply in love with his Queen, Eleanor. The chronicler Matthew Paris enthusiastically noted vices, such as one day when Edward and his bodyguard mutilated a peasant they encountered on the road, simply for the fun of torturing him.

For a time Edward improved with age, becoming conscientious and self-disciplined. Frugal eating and drinking habits kept him slim and fit. His manner was grave, courteous and frank and he made a good impression on his subjects. He shared his army's hardships on campaigns till he was over sixty. He was a committed Christian, going on the required Crusade to Jerusalem.

He lived in interesting times. With the Crusades ended, Marco Polo wandering between Europe and China, the Vikings gone, England could concentrate on the wool business. Her merchants grew wealthy, and universities were founded. So greedy eyes were cast on his country.

He took over government at a time of great change. Simon de Montfort, in order to gain people's cooperation, had attempted to govern with their consent and Edward liked this idea—a country should function like a human body in which all the parts worked together. From time to time he held the talking shops in Westminster Hall that came to be known as Parliaments. These were to offer advice, not to take decisions. Here, wrote a contemporary, 'justice is done to everyone according to his deserts'. Edward is credited with important developments in English law, and England's experience of his reign was of innovation and justice, firm government, and the beginnings of democratic consultation. 'Warlike as a leopard', his dream was to bring all of Britain the rule of the Plantagenet dynasty. This, of course, was a perfectly sensible idea. The islands are not large, and would surely

Carlisle Castle was built to protect nothern England
from the Scots (19th-century etching)

Edward's coronation. In feudal terms this meant that, having failed to pay homage to the man who claimed overlordship of Wales, Llywelyn neither intended to obey him nor to support his wars.

It took Edward five years to annexe Wales. He starved Llywelyn into defeat. Welsh resistance effectively collapsed, to be encircled with new castlefuls of Edward's soldiers. By incarcerating their little Princess Gwenllian in an English convent for the rest of her life he extinguished the blood-line of the Welsh royal family forever. To stress his triumph Edward gave the title of Prince of Wales to a baby, his own son. His final act was to abstract the Stigmata, special treasures and relics of Wales, and parade them in mockery throughout other parts of Britain.

Edward had subdued Wales, but what of Scotland? His motto was 'I keep my promise'— and he had sworn to take the whole of Britain.

Scotland was a more daunting proposition. For centuries it had had its own line of royal kings, with all that implied in a feudal ruler's mind. No mere chieftain was in charge. Geographically and ethnically the country was divided: north of the Tay lived wandering herdsmen with their own language and customs, and wild tribes or clans who were to continue warring with one another for another four hundred years, unaffected by continental customs such as feudalism. But the rolling hills and lowlands south of the Forth-Clyde line were farmed by families descended from sixth century English settlers and Normans, their feudal system and ways of life were not unlike those in England, and many great families—the Balliols and the Bruces for example—held land in both countries and so had no interest in war. Up to that time, while there had been persistent territorial squabbles in the border area, there had been little deep-seated antagonism between the two countries.

benefit from co-operation. Why waste energy on strife? Why risk the possibility of a disaffected section inviting in your enemies, such as the Norsemen or the French, by the back door? While he was busy bringing law and order to England, the Celtic fringes were in constant turmoil. First Edward made an abortive attempt to subdue Ireland, whose seaway protected her. Next an opportunity arose for him to tackle Wales. With their Celtic language and laws, the Welsh were aliens. The powerful and charismatic Llywelyn, who had strong-armed most of the north-west of his country into some sort of unity, must be quelled, for he had 'missed'

The 13th century had been particularly peaceful, helped by two dynastic marriages. Edward's aunt Joan wed Alexander II King of Scots, and his sister Margaret was Alexander III's first Queen. But when Margaret died and was replaced by a Frenchwoman, Yolande of Dreux in 1285, Edward saw Scotland drawing dangerously close to its old ally France.

Possibly the temptation to subjugate Scotland was simply too great for Edward when, one stormy March night the following year, opportunity once again favoured him. Alexander III fell from his horse and was killed, leaving no adult heir. There was a brief lull while the Scots waited to see if Yolande would produce a posthumous heir. None appeared. Edward, still the good modern thinker full of the best intentions, proposed a marriage between his heir and Alexander's little grand-daughter the Maid of Norway, at the Treaty of Birgham. When she died there was no-one left to offer.

In an apparent effort to keep Scotland from tearing itself apart, Edward went north to advise on how the rival claims to their throne should be resolved. A ruler had to be found. At that time no form of government except feudalism existed. It was essential to have a lord-superior at the top of the social and economic pyramid—otherwise the whole edifice, which depended on homage and fealty, would collapse. Edward did genuinely regard himself as overlord of Scotland, and there were good historical reasons for this. He even reinforced this by commissioning research in the monastic chronicles.

The year 1290 was a particularly dreadful one for fifty-two year-old Edward. His beloved Eleanor suddenly died. Her untimely death had a terrible effect on his personality, turning him into an embittered and savage man. Put out by the failure of his plan to annexe Scotland at a time when he needed to concentrate on foreign issues, exasperated by the persistence of the

Scottish problem, he travelled up to Norham on the river Tweed in May the following year to hold a Great Council. There, he persuaded the Scots to recognise his rights of overlordship at least during the hearings and discussions about which of the thirteen claimants to the throne would win. The possibility of gaining control of the whole of Britain must have seemed very real to Edward then.

Professor Duncan writes: 'There is no doubt that Edward's court tried to hear fairly the various claims put forward', and he appears to have gone to a great deal of trouble to listen to advice, from learned people, churchmen and foreign lawyers. There was even a record of all the proceedings of The Great Cause, as the hearings came to be called, made by a public notary. Yet, while he appeared to be acting so impartially as both judge and jury at Norham, he ordered his fleet north, to lurk about off Holy Island (Lindisfarne) ready to blockade the Scottish ports. He summoned his army from the north of England, and his treasurer suddenly started being difficult about debts owed to the crown. In the end he stated baldly that he was overlord of Scotland, challenged the Scots to disprove it if they could, and took over ownership of the royal castles. For reasons of common sense he chose John Balliol—a man who, as an English baron, owed allegiance to him, but who was of royal Scots descent. He was to be king only if he would pay homage to Edward as overlord of Scotland. And so John Balliol was inaugurated on the Stone of Destiny at Scone on St Andrews Day, 30th November 1292, accordingly going to Newcastle to pay homage to Edward as overlord of Scotland on 26th December.

'Toom Tabard' (empty coat), as Balliol came to be known, was a mere glove puppet to Edward's hand in Scottish affairs and Edward had him running up and down to London like a lackey, on idiotic whims. It was when Balliol eventually

Norham castle, Northumbria, which Edward I used as a base.

lost patience and rebelled against him that Edward lost the remnants of his humanity.

Scotland, Edward's vassal state, was to be brought to heel. In 1296 the might of the English army, with its deady longbows, was marched north to quell them once and for all, pausing only to make an example of the people at Berwick. The English sacked the prosperous little town and put 17,000 people to death, leaving their bodies to rot as a stinking threat to any other would-be rebels north of the border. It took his army some time to conquer their way to Edinburgh, but Edward finally arrived there in June. The Castle was well defended, but in the end it yielded and thereafter Edward's journey was little more than a triumphal march.

By the end of the year, his objectives apparently achieved, he returned to London, with John Balliol a prisoner bound for exile to France. Edward, now aged 57, ruled Scotland. From Edinburgh, he ordered the Scottish regalia taken to London, along with the Scottish emblem of kingship, the Stone of Destiny from Scone, which was to be installed as a trophy of war at Westminster Abbey.

Practically every book of English history that deals with this period mentions the legend of the Stone of Destiny. By taking it away, Edward believed he had won a psychological victory that would be more effective than all his abortive wars. From now on he, Edward King of England, would crush the Scots' ambitions of sovereignty, whenever he felt like it, and his heirs after him.

The Stone which arrived in London is described by the Royal Commission On Historical Monuments, London, as 'A quarry dressed block of coarse grained old red sandstone, measuring 26 1/2 inches by 16 1/2 inches by 11 inches thick. On it is a roughly incised cross, and an oblong indentation. It is fitted at the ends with iron staples, carrying rings which are so attached that a pole can easily be passed through them to facilitate carrying it. These cuttings are probably of the time of Edward I'. No expense was to be spared, and accordingly Edward ordered his goldsmith to make a fair bronze chair to contain it.

While the Abbey was closed to the public before the Coronation in 1953, the Ministry of Works took the time to examine it in detail. The workmanship and the actual materials used in the making of the chair were X-rayed, chemically analysed and minutely measured. No detail was overlooked. Lengthy and exhaustive reports were written, notes were added, and the whole lot was published by the Ministry of Works in 1953.

The Coronation Chair which still stands in

In 845 the monks of Lindisfarne took refuge from the Vikings at St Cuthbert's Church, Norham. In 1292 Edward I arbitrated the claim of the Scottish nobles here, finally selecting John Balliol.

Westminster Abbey today has been used in almost all English coronations since that of Edward II in 1307. We are told it was made by Walter of Durham in 1299 when, it is thought, he must have been aged about seventy. Walter had been the Kings' Sergeant Painter since 1270. According to the Wardrobe Accounts for 1300 he was paid one hundred shillings for the Chair, 13s 4d for the carving and painting of two wooden leopards—Kings of England during that period liked being shown with their feet resting on leopards, perhaps to model their throne on descriptions of King Solomon's throne which had 'two lions standing by the stays'— and £1 19s 7d for making a step and case for it. The earliest manuscript illustration showing the Chair dates from the early 14th century and is owned by Corpus Christi College, Cambridge. Its first appearance on a Royal Seal engraved for Edward III in 1327 when for the first time the Chair, being new and grand, receives more attention from the engraver than does the King.

But in spite of Edward Plantagenet's original order for a bronze chair, none of the research so far carried out by historians and scientists has revealed a single trace of bronze in the Chair that Walter the Painter made so beautifully for him. Why not? Did Edward realise at some point that the Stone he looted from Scone was not the Stone of Destiny? And if so, did he deliberately cover this up to save face? Certainly he always appears to have treated the Stone he brought from Scotland with respect. It is listed in several inventories of his most choice possessions, as *Una petra magna super quam Reges Scociae solebatt coronari* (a large stone on which Scottish Kings were crowned). He was a most devout man—as well as a superstitious one—he carried sacred relics about on his person, such as his two pieces of the original Calvary rock.

However the ungrateful Scots would not lie down and accept defeat. Aged sixty-eight, his health and strength exhausted, still obsessed with the conviction that he owned Scotland, and that the English army, God and his royal self would grind the Scottish people under his heel, this once respected monarch died in July, 1307, demanding with his last gasp that his dead bones be carried into Scotland at the head of the English army, and that his tombstone would bear the epitaph Edward *Malleus Scottorum*, Hammer of the Scots.

[Berwick.]

Engraving by J.W. Whimper

14. Wallace and the Missing Stone

The end of the thirteenth century was a crucial period in the story of the Stone of Destiny, for it was then that it disappeared from the written history of Scotland, only to reappear in the oral tradition. So that we can attempt to work out which of the ensuing legends is nearest to the truth, some scrutiny of the events, the attitudes and the mood of Scots at that time is necessary.

On 18th March 1286 Alexander III galloped homeward from an Edinburgh party to Fife where his young queen Yolande awaited him. There was a terrible storm and next morning he was found on the shore below Kinghorn cliffs, dead. The fourteenth century poet and scholar John Barbour expressed the feelings of Scots at that time:

> 'Sen Alexander our king wes deid
> That Scotland left in luve and lee,
> Away wes sonse of aill and breid,
> Of wine and wax, of gamin and glee.
> The gold wes changit all in leid,
> The frute failyeit on everilk tree,
> Christ succour Scotland and remeid
> That stad is in perplexitie.'

Scots were indeed in trouble. The Maid of Norway died on her way to Scotland. In desperation, as we have seen, they invited their ally, King Edward I, as a well-known modern thinker, to arbitrate. For eighty years there had been peace and prosperity between Scotland and England connected by trade, by nobles with lands in both, and by dynastic marriage. But when Edward turned up at Norham that May of 1291, they were amazed to discover a self-styled Lord Paramount.

Fordun describes the day, 17 November, when John Balliol was proclaimed King, 'The Earl of Gloucester, holding Robert the Bruce by the hand, in the sight of all, spoke thus to the king: 'Recollect O King what kind of judgement thou hast given today and know that thou must be judged at the last, and straightaway at the Earl's bidding the aforesaid Robert Bruce withdrew, nor did he ever tender homage or fealty to John of Balliol'. Balliol knelt before Edward after his coronation on St Andrew's Day, 30 November 1292, the last recorded inauguration of a Scottish King on the Stone of Destiny, having sold his country for a crown.

According to feudal theory, the relationship between England and Scotland should now have been of mutual benefit—Edward's overlordship implying not only submission to him by the Scottish people, but also his responsibility for their protection.

Balliol's press has traditionally been bad. Only his blood was Scottish. His life experience, lands and loves had all been in France and England. Historian Michael Lynch cites; 'dispensation of justice on an unusual scale . . . and consultation with the political community in parliament as well as council' as features of his reign, so he may not have been such a bad man. As we have seen, Edward proceeded to turn him into a figure of ridicule, yet, with quiet courage better suited to a Shakespearian hero than his weak image suggests, Balliol rebelled. He made an alliance with Philip IV of France, accused Edward of having 'caused harm beyond measure to the liberties of ourselves and our kingdom', and renounced his fealty and homage 'which, be it said, were extorted by extreme coercion on your part'.

This is what brought Edward raging north with his army in 1296. On 30th March they hit Berwick. He ordered that none were to be spared. It took three days to kill every man woman and child and for weeks their bloated corpses were left to rot. Thus began a chapter of unsurpassed violence in Scottish history that would go down in posterity as the Wars of Independence, which were to last for almost 200 years, and which blackened the relationship between the two nations for many centuries.

While the bodies were still hanging from the windows and stinking in the gutters, Edward summoned the Scottish nobility to the town to sign what came to be known as the 'Ragman Rolls'. 1,500 were forced, in that unforgettable atmosphere, to acknowledge his 'superiority'. Perhaps one understands why Balliol might have preferred civilised alliance with France to servitude as this tyrant's vassal. Later the dead were shovelled into pits in order to repopulate the town with English incomers. Striking north, making no secret of his intentions, Edward took town after town—Dunbar, Stirling, Perth, then Brechin. At Montrose he had John Balliol dragged before him in chains.

Nigel Tranter colours in the bleak outlines: the scene is Stracathro Church near Brechin Cathedral, the date 10th July. Present, various ecclesiastics, Robert Bruce—now twenty-two, some

men-at-arms. Edward 1, in his late fifties, wearing armour, clatters up to the Altar on his horse. Eight men drag in John Balliol King of Scots, 'he wore no armour but . . . a most gorgeous tabard . . . heraldically embroidered in blazing colours, picked out in gold and rubies, depicting, back and front, the red Rampant Lion of Scotland on a tressured field of yellow . . . The man was limping slightly, and being tall, had obvious difficulty in adjusting his stride to the short chain of the the leg-irons which clamped his ankles'.

He is followed by John Comyn, also shackled, carrying the Crown of Scotland and the Sceptre of the Realm. Edward yawns and delegates the business to Bishop Anthony Bek. Comyn tries to speak up for Balliol and is silenced by a blow from Bek's mailed fist. The crown and sceptre fall to the floor. Bek 'stepping close . . . reached out and took hold of the splendid . . . tabard . . . grabbing it at the neck . . . To the sound of rending fabric its wearer staggered, and as the glorious garment fell in ruin to the floor, some thing of the light and colour seemed to go out of that place'.

Edward had the Great Seal of the Guardians publicly smashed. His recorded words were: 'A man does good business when he rids himself of a turd'. He then struck north, reaching Aberdeen a week later. All Scotland knew of his presence, his purpose, and his intention to take the Stone of Destiny. Averaging about twelve miles a day, he was across the Spey by Tuesday 24th July, turning south to reach Brechin by Saturday 5th August. The Abbot of Aberbrothock had been preaching subversive propaganda to his flock— 'there was but women and no men in England'. The churchmen of Scotland were not afraid of Edward.

By Wednesday 8th August 1296 Edward 1 was at St John's of Perth. Between 5th and 8th August a Stone was wrenched from Scone Abbey by Edward's men—a Stone reputed to be the 'Palladium of Scotland', on which Balliol and all the Scottish Kings before him had been crowned. *'Apud Monasterium de Scone positus erat lapis pergrandis in ecclesia Dei, juxta magnum altare, concavus quidem ad modum rotundae cathedrae confectus, in quo futur reges loc quasi coronationis ponebantur exmore . . .'* (at Scone monastery was an unusually large stone in God's church, beside the high Altar, concave like a round decorated chair in which kings would be crowned), and at Edinburgh Castle, 1296, arrived *'una petra magna super quam Reges Scotieae solebant coronari'* (a large stone on which Scottish Kings were crowned). In Edward's wardrobe accounts for 1300 is a payment to Walter the Painter for the new chair *'in qua petra Scocie reponitur juxta altare ante feretrum Sancit Edwardi in Ecclesia Abbatie Westmonaster'*—in which the Scottish stone lies beside St Edward's Altar in Westminster Abbey.

In a 'parliament' Edward demanded Scots' obedience as his subjects. Scotland was now an English colony.

For the first time in Scottish history, the people were moved to unite fully against a predator— and the catalyst was the younger son of a Renfrewshire laird. His name was William Wallace. This large, unflinching and charismatic young man appeared from nowhere in 1297 to galvanise anti-English feeling into organised revolt in Scotland.

In his novel *Wallace* (1975), Tranter conjures up the sort of scene Scots were being forced to witness. Wallace comes upon Carleith Tower in Ayrshire one hot summer's day:

All the cottar-folk, farmhands, shepherds, cattlemen, wrights, smith, miller and the rest, of a little self-contained community amongst these Ayrshire-Lanarkshire border hills, with their families, had been driven in here, to their laird's courtyard, and slaughtered en masse ...their bodies crammed down the well, where the lairdly family had been elevated on ropes. There might be thirty or forty or more, in that well.'

Dead bodies were none so rare a sight in the Scotland of 1296 admittedly, but these were exceptional. When the drawbridge was let down, the portcullis apparatus here projected two long timber beams, from which the chains depended. These beams had been used as gibbets . . . There were fourteen bodies, or parts of bodies, swaying gently on ropes. Old Cunninghame of Carleith himself, the laird . . . hung . . . from the keystone of the arched gateway . . . by an ankle . . . his white-bearded head . . . kicked into a corner.

But it was the women who had them all but vomiting. Lady Carleith . . .her three daughters and two serving women had all suffered alike . . . All hung upside-down, naked; all had their breasts sliced off; and all had stakes or axe-shafts or other wooden handles projecting upwards from between their thighs . . . Five children . . . aged from two to eight, had merely been hacked to pieces and the parts strung up anyhow, in bundles. The flies were a humming dark cloud about all.

Wallace himself had no ambition to sit on the Stone of Destiny, he never wanted to become King—his aim was to restore John Balliol. But after beating the English at Stirling Bridge and a raid on an English court at Scone in 1297, he was persuaded to become Guardian of Scotland. A year later he was defeated at Falkirk, and outlawed. His exploits caught the imagination and heart of Robert the Bruce, who decided he must now join the fight for the nation in which he was born, and Wallace resigned in favour of the joint Guardianship of Bruce and John Comyn. Through treachery Wallace was caught and most cruelly executed according to Edward's command on 24th August 1305 in London. His mutilated body was distributed for display in Newcastle, Berwick, Stirling and Perth.

15. Robert the Bruce

Robert the Bruce is an important figure in the story of the Stone of Destiny. The description of his inaugurations are ambiguous—was he or was he not crowned upon a stone chair of enthronment? Only by weighing up the evidence and looking at the man himself can we begin to make judgements about what he may have done with it.

Robert the Bruce was born on 11 July 1274 at Turnberry Castle in the idyllic south-west of Scotland. A lightouse now blinks from its ruins towards the nearby shore of Ulster, and Bruce seems always to have had an affinity for this particular seaway and the Clyde estuary. He first appears in history aged twelve, witnessing a deed of Alexander Macdonald of Islay in the Paisley *registrum*. We hear nothing more until he is eighteen, but it is clear that he was thoroughly educated, physically strong, well-trained in fighting skills, and a well-rounded, likeable individual.

How and why Robert the Bruce became King of Scots is ground that has been well raked over by scores of historians, poets and novelists—every tourist knows of persevering spiders in caves. Here we merely search for sufficient understanding to help lead us to the Stone of Destiny.

Bruce was ambitious. His royal blood came down the female line from Kenneth MacAlpin. A lowland lord of Norman descent, Bruce's allegiance was uncertain to start with, but by age twenty-two, a decision had to be made.

Edward had marched off south about his business in 1296, believing Scotland was conquered, not bothering to consolidate his victory. Historian Michael Lynch explains in his new history *Scotland* (1991) how this failure was symptomatic of the failure of Edward's regime. Conquest and conciliation worked against each other; 'Forfeiture of lands in Scotland was a necessary device to compensate the English earls and captains who remained mostly unpaid for their part in the Scottish campaigns; but a lasting reconciliation of disaffected Scottish nobles could be achieved only by a generous regrant of their lands.'

The two Guardians had the most to gain. Never the best of friends, Bruce and Comyn had only been persuaded to work together with difficulty. In October came the news that Edward 1 was ill. He might die. Bruce offered Comyn a deal. Either you help me onto the throne in return for my estates, or you give me yours and I'll help you become King. Comyn opted for land, and they exchanged signed indentures. Bruce was to be King. Meanwhile Edward made

opposite Remains of Turnberry Castle

a miraculous recovery. In January 1306, Bruce and Comyn were in London. Comyn gave his copy of the deal to Edward, then raced homeward to Dumfries. Edward presented the indenture to Bruce, demanding 'Was it sealed by thee?' According to A.A.H. Douglas's translation of Barbour, Bruce replied:

> What simple fool I be!
> Not always is my seal with me.
> I have a man that bears the seal;
> And therefore, if it be your will,
> I ask respite that I may better
> Become acquainted with this letter.

HERE STOOD THE MONASTERY OF THE GREY FRIARS WHERE ON THURSDAY 10TH FEBRUARY 1306 ROBERT THE BRUCE AIDED BY SIR ROGER KIRKPATRICK SLEW THE RED COMYN AND OPENED THE FINAL STAGE OF THE WAR FOR SCOTTISH INDEPENDENCE WHICH ENDED VICTORIOUSLY ON THE FIELD OF BANNOCKBURN 1314 "I MAK SICCAR" ERECTED BY THE CITIZENS OF DUMFRIES & THE SALTIRE SOCIETY.

> Tomorrow when you take your seat,
> And all your lords together meet,
> This letter shall I hither bear,
> That all your parliament may hear,
> And as security I pledge
> All lands that are my heritage . . .

Bruce hurries home to his lodgings and sends for his clerk;

> The Bruce bad fetch without delay
> Two sturdy horses to the door.
> He and the clerk , and no-one more,
> Leapt on the horses, all unseen;
> And day and night, with nought between
> They rode till in Lochmaben town
> The fifth day out they lighted down . .

> 'It chanced that on that very day
> Within Dumfries, not far away,
> Sir John the Comyn made abode.
> The Bruce took horse and thither rode,
> Intent that he should speedily
> Avenge the other's treachery.

> He lost no time and, hurrying on,
> At Greyfriars he found Sir John
> Beside the altar; lightly spoke,
> And showed him, as it were a joke,
> The signed indenture; then with a knife
> Right on the spot he reft his life!

> Doubt not, it was a great misdeed
> Of holy altar to take no heed!
> Thereby such hardship Bruce befell
> That nee'er in story heard I tell
> Of any man had such distress
> Before he won to his success.

The thirty-one year-old Bruce was now in a most awkward situation.

His decision was instant. He went straight to Glasgow to seek absolution from little old Bishop

Wishart, who granted it, and sent word out around the country to that effect, telling the clergy to rally to Bruce as though to a sacred cause. In return Bruce promised to preserve and defend the Scottish Church. Spiritually more at ease, he sent a formal demand to Edward 1 that he was to be recognised as King of Scots—and an urgent message to Bishop Lamberton to head for Scone without delay to crown him.

So, one March morning, a small procession set out from Lochmaben, skirting the loch and wending its way a hundred miles northwards through the flowers of springtime, to Scone. Tranter writes;

> A company of mounted instumentalists and minstrels led the procession, dispensing sweet music; banners fluttered by the score; gorgeously-caparisoned horses, heraldically-emblazoned litters, silks, satins, velvets and jewellery, dazzled the eye. Bruce himself wore a cloth-of-gold tabard, with the Lion of Scotland embroidered in red front and rear, picked out in rubies, and his queen was in royal purple velvet..

Bishop Lamberton sent his young protegee James Douglas ahead of him from Berwick, then under cover of darkness, rode direct to Scone. The poet Barbour has Douglas meeting Bruce near Arickstone, and bowing low, saying he had come to do homage to him as rightful King and to share his fortunes, and Bruce knighting him there and then. The resulting friendship was to last throughout his life. The ordinary people had greeted Bruce with enthusiasm but, says Tranter, they had 'little to lose, and at this stage not a great deal to contribute'. The landed nobles, knights and lairds, who alone could provide Bruce with armed forces, money and horses, held back, waiting to see, after ten years of warfare with England, what would happen. Bishop Wishart brought out the the vestments of kingship he had hidden. It is unlikely that the vestments were the only items to have been stashed away.

Tranter has the Abbot, a small and cheery cleric of considerable age, leading Bruce and Lamberton down into the 'damp and dripping vaults', unlocking a door and, lifting his lantern high, triumphantly revealing the Stone of Destiny.

Details which have come down to us about the ceremony that took place at Scone on 25th March 1306 are tantalisingly brief. The vestments were placed around Bruce's shoulders. A simple circlet of gold was placed on his head. Lamberton anointed him with oil. He did sit on what is described as the Coronation Chair. Did it contain the Stone of Destiny, brought out of hiding for

Bruce held a parliament in St John's Church, Ayr, in 1315.

83

the occasion by the spirited little Abbott who had been in charge when Edward's men had come to take it away?

There is one unusual circumstance about Bruce's coronation. Noticeably absent was the young McDuff, Earl of Fife, traditionally the person charged with the duty of placing the crown on the head of the King of Scots. He was being held in England as a ward of Court. But Isabel, his nineteen-year-old sister, had heard about the coronation. She was married to the Earl of Buchan—an ally of Edward and kinsman of the dead Comyn. In spite of taking the Earl's best horse, and galloping towards Scone, she missed Bruce's coronation by a day.

Facing excommunication, Bruce was keen to have as many of the parts of the ceremony working for him as possible, so he arranged to go through a second coronation ceremony on Palm Sunday, forty-eight hours after the first, and for this, Isabel lifted the golden circlet and placed it on his brow, and he was truly King of Scots according to every tradition.

Members of the English court, who found it inconceivable that a woman could have a higher motive than sex for her actions, decided her dash to Bruce's side at Scone must mean she was his mistress. To thank her, Bruce's Queen Elizabeth took Isabel into her household as a lady-in-waiting. But when later that year they were captured, along with Bruce's sister Mary, at Tain, Edward I had them shut up in wooden cages like animals and exposed to public ridicule, Mary at Roxburgh Castle, and Isabel on the ramparts at Berwick. There they remained for *four years*. They barely survived. Meanwhile Bruce's daughter, the twelve year-old Marjorie, was caged in the Tower of London, and Queen Elizabeth was shut away in a convent.

The Pope not only excommunicated Bruce for his murder of the Comyn in Greyfriars Kirk, but placed an Interdict on Scotland. Bruce may have been crowned King of Scots, but he had yet to persuade many people to come round to him, and to regain freedom for them. It took many years, during which he was hunted high and low. He kept on the move between Ireland, Carrick and Kyle, the Western Highlands and Islands. A brief respite came when Edward 1 died. Bruce ruled wisely, and became well-loved by his people.

Eventually, in March 1324, Bruce heard that Edward II was coming to 'save' Stirling Castle, garrisoned by English, and under serious seige by Bruce's brother. At midsummer the two armies met near the Bannock Burn, within view of the castle. Six thousand Scots miraculously defeated twenty thousand English. Such was the panic that Edward II lost his shield, his privy seal, and even his court poet, who was forced thereafter to compose victory verses for the Scots.

The Bannockburn victory established Bruce's authority. For his day he proved remarkably merciful. Prisoners were exchanged, and his long suffering Queen Elizabeth, young Marjory and Mary came home. Of Isabel there is no mention in the list of returnees. She may have died in a Carmelite nunnery to which she'd been sent. She can't have been more than twenty-seven.

Till then, Elizabeth did not have a relaxed life. Married to Bruce in her teens, imprisoned for years, she never knew if her husband was alive or dead. Bruce built a manor for them at Cardross, near Dumbarton on the Clyde. There they set out a garden, an aviary for their falcons and a slip for their boat. He could keep an eye on his navy at Dumbarton. Even so, they took six years to produce an heir. Bruce's problems were made immeasurably more difficult by the Pope's sanctions. For the sake of the economy and his own immortal soul, Bruce needed to have them lifted. Arbroath Abbey was his administrative centre where Church affairs were headed by

Lamberton, affairs of State by his Chancellor, Abbott of Arbroath Bernard of Linton. The Declaration of Arbroath was probably written there with Bernard's supervision, perhaps by Alexander Kinninmonth, who was to take this persuasive document to the Pope in Avignon. Sealed by eight earls and thirty-one barons, and in the name of the community of the realm, it was sent on its way in April 1320. Stressing the ecclesiastical goodness of Scots, it tells how Scots dwelt in freedom and quietness till Edward 1 invaded their country in the guise of an ally.

> At length it pleased God . . . to restore us to liberty . . . by our most serene prince, King and Lord, Robert . . . and the due and lawful consent and assent of all the people made him our King and prince. To him we are obliged and resolved to adhere in all things . . . as being the person who has restored the people's safety, in defence of their liberties. But, after all, if this prince shall leave these principles he has so nobly pursued and consent that we of our Kingdom be subjected to the King of people of England, we will immediately endeavour to expel him as our enemy . . . for so long as there shall be but one hundred of us remain alive we will never give consent to subject ourselves to the dominion of the English. For it is not glory, it is not riches, neither is it honour, but it is freedom alone that we fight and contend for, which no honest man will lose but with his life'.

The writers reminded the Pope that, since he himself would eventually be judged , would he please tell the King of England to be content with what he had. There is also a firm sentence about how the Pope's conscience will be answerable for all the blood and 'loss of souls and other calamities' if he allows the warring to go on. It is difficult to convey the quiet, well-argued insistence of the tone of this Declaration in these snatches, but it gives evidence of how the people felt about Bruce. To an extent it worked. The

The head of Bruce at Bannockburn was modelled from the skull discovered at Dunfermline Abbey.

Pope sent a stern letter to Edward 11, and soon officially recognised Bruce as King. There came a few peaceful years. Bruce thanked the Church, and the families who had helped him with land grants, including Angus Og, Lord of the Isles. He made grants for the reconstruction of Melrose Abbey. So much did he spend that he had to ask a Parliament at Cambuskenneth Abbey in July 1326 for an increase in his income. It was given, and his son David was formally recognised as his successor.

Elizabeth died on 26 October 1327. By age fifty-six Bruce's own health was beginning to deteriorate. His illness has been labelled leprosy, but a more recent diagnosis of his sypmtoms suggests scurvy, a disease caused, as we now know, by an inadequate intake of vitamin C, causing haemorrhages, infection and pain. Bruce became anxious to make his peace with God.

He spent this time pottering about his gardens and sailing on the Clyde. The Pope at last lifted his Interdict on Scotland and his excommunication from Bruce, who set off on his last pilgrimage, to the shrine of St Ninian at Whithorn.

In May 1329 the peace concluded at Edinburgh was ratified by the English Parliament and at last came acknowledgement of the independence of Scotland 'separate in all things from the kingdom of England'. This was welded by the marriage of two children, David aged four, and Edward 111's sister Joan who was seven.

King Robert the Bruce lay down to die, summoning his friends to his bedside. He explained that his illness was his penance for all the suffering he had caused others in his wars, and that he had made a vow to God that if he should manage to secure peace for his realm he would go on a crusade. Now that he couldn't, would one of them please take his heart to the holy sepulchre in Jerusalem. James Douglas was chosen.

In the Bruce Trilogy Tranter dramatises the situation enticingly: Bruce makes Angus Og of the Isles 'dewar' of the Stone of Destiny. Bruce has made his farewells to most of his friends, and now it is the turn of Angus Og of the Isles. Bruce makes him 'dewar' of the Stone of Destiny. 'After my son's coronation. Take it to your Isles, where none shall be able to follow it. And keep it safe, on some fair island. Until one of my line, or whoever is true King of Scots, requires it again for coronation.'

When Bruce expired on 7th June 1329 his body was embalmed and his heart extracted and given to Sir James before the remains were carried in a splendid funeral procession across Scotland to Dunfermline Abbey for interrment.

'And when the people knew that King Robert was dead, the sound of sorrow went from place to place.'

Douglas set Bruce's heart in an enamelled silver casket slung round his neck. He did go crusading, with six other knights, but was killed when the Moors attacked their expedition in Spain. Bruce's heart was brought home along with Douglas's bones. Douglas was buried in the Kirk of Douglas, and Bruce's heart beneath the High Altar at Melrose Abbey. Professor Barrow describes Bruce as 'a potentate in the immemorial mould of the western Gaidhealtachd, inured since youth to a rough country and to rough warfare on land and sea . . . his grasp of tactics and strategy show him to have been much more than a guerilla leader, his governance was characterised by patience and a sense of justice . . . his picture of Scotland in the world was truly international, and his character had a peaceable, compassionate and humorous side which cannot but make those who read the sources warm to the man'.

In the Reformation all the tombs in Dunfermline Abbey were destroyed, but during the course of building work the skeleton of a large man was exhumed, the breast-bone cut away as for the extraction of the heart. A plaster cast of the skull was made and built into a head. At Melrose, an embalmed heart was removed from beneath the High Altar and transferred, for some strange reason, to the gardens beyond. Today Robert the Bruce rides his bronze horse in triumph over the field of Bannockburn, his bones buried in Dumfermline Abbey, his heart beneath the green lawns of Melrose, and his lips forever sealed on the question of what he knows about the Stone of Destiny.

PART IV

16. Lord of the Isles

After 1296 the Stone of Destiny leaves history and passes again into tradition and legend, cropping up in the folklore of several places in Scotland.

Early in the Spring following Robert the Bruce's death as we have seen in the previous chapter, a party of his friends led by Sir James Douglas left for the Crusades. But one was absent—Angus Og of Islay. As we have seen, it is believed by some that Bruce, well aware that Scotland was in for another long regency, had asked him to take the Stone of Destiny into hiding.

Angus Og inherited Kintyre and Mull, but his brothers were either Comyn supporters or greedy for land. During Bruce's lifetime John MacDougall of Lorn, Comyn's son-in-law and proprietor of Dunollie and Dunstaffnage, had taken the opportunity of ambushing Bruce and his followers as they fled westward soon after the inauguration ceremony, through the narrow Pass of Brander in Argyll. Bruce only just escaped. Till then, he had been unsure of Angus Og's allegiance, but Angus arranged for a ship to spirit Bruce safely down the Clyde and handed over Dunaverty Castle to him, later persuading him to head for safety to Rathlin Island, off the north coast of Ireland. Angus's loyalty was tested. In revenge, John of Lorn ambushed Angus on his way to Mull. The following tale resulted, rediscovered and treasured today by Danny Campbell of Bowmore, Islay.

There isn't enough space for all of James Fyfe's ballad 'Donald O' Islay' (for Donald read Angus), but a few stanzas give a flavour of it.

O the castle yett is steekit fast
An' sair tae speel is the castle wa';
Ahint them deep i' the dungeon cast
Lies Donald o' Islay, aince sae braw.

His raven locks are matted wi' gore,
His face is wan an' haggart an' worn;
Fu' length he lies on the cauld earth floor,
The wounded prisoner o' John o' Lorn.

The clansmen o' Lorn had ambush laid
I' the darkest neuk o' a lanesome glen,
Wi' hearts fu' o' veneance lang they stayed
Tae slay the noble Bruce an' his men.

An' first i' the Bruce's band sae sma'
Gaed Donald o' Islay brave an' true;
He led the gair, aye foremaist o' a',
Whaur red bluid flows an' whaur swords gleam blue.

The fighting is detailed till the last moment, when:

An arrow had pierced his shouther deep,
An' he swooned awa' an' kent nae mair
Till he cam' tae i' the darksome keep,
Streek'd stiff an' sair on the earthen flair.

Thrown into John of Lorn's deepest dungeon at Dunstaffnage, Angus languishes there till one day he is visited by the beautiful Sheila of Auchindell. She tells him she's being forced to wed Ian of Lorn, and that on her wedding day Angus is to be hanged—but takes him into her care anyway and nurses him back to health. She gazes up at him with her 'een sae blue' and whispers that she'd have preferred him for her bridegroom.

Then e'en as she spak', the soun' o' arms
On the castle wa's an' yett broke loose,
An' clear aboon a' the loud alarms
Rang the battle-cry 'A Bruce, A Bruce.'

Syne the chamber door was opened wide
An' Donald sank tae his bended knee,
For staun'in' there on the step ootside
Was the kingly Bruce, sae fair tae see.

An' a smile played owre his noble face:
Tae Donald he spak', an' thus spak' he:
'I've risked my life tae reach this place
I' the hope that I micht rescue thee,

'But I find ye noo' in bondage held
Faur stronger than Lorn could ever bind,
For nae chains that foe could ever weld
Can haud like the love o' woman kind.

'But quick through the glen we a' maun gang,
An' swift owre the muir we a' maun ride,
For I wou'dna' like tae see ye hang
Ere ye made this lady fair your bride.

Bruce accompanies them thence to Islay where they are wed.

Angus did become one of Bruce's most loyal friends, and, in thanks, Bruce passed Islay and the chieftainship of Clan Donald to him, and Angus thus became not his subject, but a near equal, supporting Bruce of his own free will. After the success of Bannockburn, at which Angus Og fought well, Bruce rewarded him with more islands, along with Ardnamurchan, Glencoe, and part of Lochaber. Kintyre he kept for his own son. According to Fordun, Angus Og *Ri Innse Gall* (King of the Isles of the Strangers) had two residences on Islay; his stronghold, Dunivaig

Castle, protected the south-west, and his hideaway fastness in Finlaggan Loch was the place of inauguration and the centre of government for almost two centuries thereafter. The Stone of Destiny could have been kept in either. Dean Monro described how the Lords of the Iles often held counsel on the 'Ile of Finlaggan,' and that it had been traditionally constructed, with 'ane fair chapell.' Only 'ane pennystane cast' away there was another, smaller, island 'callit in Irish Ellan na comharle,' on which was built the actual counsel house, in which fourteen 'Barons' 'decernit, decreitit and gave suits furth upon all debaitable matters according to the Laws.' He

The top layers of building have to be carefully examined before lower and
much older layers can be investigated.

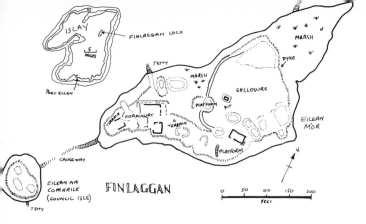

FINLAGGAN

ISLAY
FINLAGGAN LOCH
5 MILES
PORT ELLEN
MARSH
JETTY
MARSH
DYKE
ENCLOSURE
PLATFORM
PIT
FORECOURT
TERRACE
EILEAN MOR
PLATFORM
EILEAN NA COMHAILE (COUNCIL ISLE)
CAUSEWAY
JETTY
0   50   100   150   200
FEET

noted that in their day 'thair was great peace and welth in the Iles throw the ministration of justice.'

But the Stone Table around which they sat was 'carried away by Argyle with the bells that were at Icolumkill (Iona)'. This has been identified as the result of an expedition to Islay by the Marquess of Argyll about 1642. Other writers mention a Stone 2.1 metres square, bearing a footprint.

On Islay today Dr David Caldwell and the Finlaggan Trust are the focus of a ferment of archaeological interest as they begin several years of excavation at a new site—the stronghold of Angus' descendants the Lords of the Isles. Only two rather ambiguous stones have so far been identified on the site, but there is much digging yet to be done. Finlaggan Chapel is the best preserved of the buildings perhaps because, as the most important place, it was built on the best ground. The Council Isle, it turns out, is a crannog—a man-made island—on the end of an invisible underwater causeway discovered by Dr Caldwell in 1991. He also discovered a network of paved roads on Eilean Mor, dated easily by the find of two groats of James 111, minted in about 1485. On Eilean Mor, beneath centuries-deep turf, Dr Caldwell's team is now discovering the ruins of the Great Hall—used for feasts and when other chiefs visited—its stores and service buildings, servants quarters, two wells, guard houses by the jetty, the residence of the Lord and his family, and an enclosure which was probably

a garden. Cleanly carved graveslabs lie by the burial ground.

He works with a team of archaeologists and the Finlaggan Trust—Islay people such as retired teachers Rona and Donald McKenzie, Catriona Bell, busy editor of the local newspaper *Ileach*, and her husband Donald who farms Finlaggan, and Mhairi McIntyre, crofter and ex-editor of *Ileach*. Mhairi was thrilled to find a fragment of chain-mail. When the excavation is over some public access to this ancient centre of civilisation will be created.

'One of the 15th century graveslabs at Finlaggan has a flaw on the back of it which some believe is the foot print stone' writes Dr Caldwell. Above the western shore of the loch an outcrop of rock

Dr David Caldwell searches for a causeway on *Eilean Mor.*

90

has another faint indentation. Others argue that this was the inaugural footprint because it is in the 'living' rock. 'I live in hope that that is still to be discovered,' he says.

During the first summer, workers turned up a large and delicately worked Stone. Carved in the Iona workshops in Bruce's day or slightly later, it turned out to be the head of a cross. The discovery of a harp key especially pleased Mhairi, for it proved Islay folk were never just 'a bunch of savages'. On the contrary, they had practised and enjoyed art and music. Dr Caldwell says 'If I am right in my hunch we will find the remnants of a very rich history . . . the longest continuity of occupation we can hope to find, from pre-history up until the eighteenth-century . . . It is

Mairi McIntyre, who found a piece of chain-mail.

remarkable no serious attempt has been made to appreciate the story of Finlaggan'. He does not rule out the possibility that the Stone of Destiny may have been here, possibly used as the Council Table itself.

Angus Og operated as an Arthurian leader, his island lords around their Table. It was his son John who was first to be formally styled Lord of the Isles. It is clear that the Macdonald had enjoyed absolute power, operating a kind of 'feudo-clanship'—a mixture of landholding and kinship, and that he was inaugurated like a king, on a Stone. Only in detail was his ceremony different from that of the kings of Scots at Scone, such as that he wore a white habit, for innocence and integrity of heart, and to suggest he would be a light to his people and maintain their religion. He received a white rod intimating that he had the power to rule with discretion and sincerity, and his forefathers' sword signifying that he would protect his people. Afterwards the white robe was given to his poet, by traditional right, and the feasting went on for a week. Fragments of the literature, collected by the Dean of Lismore (1915-26) show Irish preoccupation with the old oral cycles like the stories of of Tir-nan-og the land-of-the-ever-young beyond the sunset, and praise-songs sung by the seannachies till they were proscribed as 'sorners' (beggars) in 1612.

Always there was the Celtic need for decoration, art, splendour and beauty. The Welsh historian Giraldus wrote in the 12th century that the Scots harpers were 'the genuine source of the art.' They used quills, or their fingernails grown long for the purpose, and they adorned their harps with silver and gems if possible, and those who were too poor used crystals instead. It becomes more and more inconceivable that a Stone revered by such a people would not be highly decorated and embellished.

Angus Og died at Finlaggan, not long after Bruce, in 1329. His body was taken to Iona for burial like those of his forebears. Three and a half centuries later, when the Lordship was forfeited, all their records were lost or destroyed. What happened to the Council Stone, and the Stone of Inauguration, on forfeiture? Peter Clarke wrote recently in the *Observer* about the dig: 'one of the best discoveries would be the Coronation Stone with its incised footmark. Described in medieval sources, it has since disppappeared'.

Dr Caldwell is worried in case there is any truth in the tradition which says the Campbells removed a Stone from Finlaggan at the end of the seventeenth century, when they were quelling the MacDonalds, or that the Stone may have been broken up. If so, will the fragments be found when they dig deep into the Council Isle in the coming years? Or did the Macdonalds escape with their Stone after forfeiture and tranport them in one of their famous galleys to Skye?

Danny Campbell of Bowmore treasures the poems of Islay, including 'Donald O'Islay'

above top
Dunivaig Castle

above
Eilean Mor and Eilean Comhairle

right
Standing stone on Islay

left
Dunstaffnage

below
Looking westward from the shore of Loch nam Uamh, Skye. The rock formation includes several caves

opposite
St Oran's Chapel, Iona. Oran was Columba's cousin and this is the earliest surviving building on the island. The chevron and beak-work of the doorway bears similarities to mid-12th century Irish carving.

above left The Clanranald Crest *above right* The People's Palace, Glasgow *below* Dull Church, where the Templar Stone is kept

17. The Search for the Stone of Skye

Did the Campbells have anything to do with it? At Inveraray Castle Alastair Campbell of Airds, Unicorn Pursuivant, and the Chief Executive of Clan Campbell, admits that he has heard of the disappearance of the Council Stone from Finlaggan, says there is no trace of either the stone or of tales about it at Inveraray, and reminds us that the Cambells of Cawdor became the owners of Islay in the seventeenth century.

If the Stone is not on Islay, where might it have gone? After Angus Og's descendants forfeited their Lordship they led seven major risings to restore it, but the death of Domhnall Dubh in 1545 put an end to their hopes. There remains a tradition that, when one branch of Clan Donald took over the Sleat Peninsula of Skye in the 17th century, the Stone went with them. The secret of exactly where it is kept is supposedly handed down from father to son. Stories about it variously suggest that it is kept in a cave, and/or hidden by a waterfall. The only problem about this legend is that neither the head of the Sleat Macdonald family, Sir Iain Bosville Macdonald, nor the chief of the clan, Lord Macdonald, admit to knowing anything about it. But of course they wouldn't, would they, if it's a family secret?

Armadale Castle is now the magnificent Clan Centre of the Macdonalds. No written records about the Stone have been found there. But branches of the clan are scattered over the globe,

so it was only mildly surprising to discover that, in the fifties, a series of letters was written by a young man, born in India but then living in Brighton, who claimed secret knowledge of the Skye Stone's whereabouts. This particular letter writer had just sufficient intriguing fact among his hotch-potch of information and misinformation to catch the imagination. He signed himself 'C. Iain Alasdair Macdonald.'

The excerpts from his letters are quoted as they were written, so that spelling, style and tone can be taken into consideration along with content. The first arrived in April 1959, on crested notepaper showing a rampant bird, a ship, and the motto 'per mare per terras':

I have in my possession an antique chest which has been handed down . . . through generations of Macdonalds of the Isles and which dates back to Somerled, Regulus of the Isles . . . In the secret place [on Skye] where the chest was origionally hidden is also 'The Stone' which I believe is the 'Stone of Destiny' . . . I may add that I myself am decended from Macdonalds of the Isles. My family hailing from Sleate.

The next letter said:

I am now the custodian of 'The Stone' and have seen it myself and know its hiding place in Skye. I was brought from India by my Grandfather and father to Skye and taken to

Armadale Castle, Clan Centre of the Macdonalds

the secret hiding place and shown the Stone, which I sat on and made to take the oath to guard its secret whereabouts and also to screen my successor.

'So well is it hidden that I was taken four times along the secret route and then find my own way four times to make sure I had a clear picture in my mind—of the route stone by stone. I went again myself after discharge from the forces after the war in 1946 which took me quite a while to find my way . . .

'The Stone' which measures approx 11 inches by 21 inches is supposed to be resting in its origional seating of marble but presume half of it is is missing. The Stone as far as I can make out resembles a well filled pillow and has many weird superstitions—rather amusing. My Grandfather often said its like no known stone he has ever seen and he was widly travelled. He said 'Heaven alone knows where it originated' Having seen it and sat on it, I have no doubts about it being the real thing. My mind takes me back to my first aquaintance with it and never shall I forget

the experience as I sat on it—before I knew what it really was.'

In another letter Macdonald offers his pedigree as evidence of his right to the secret of the whereabouts of the Stone of Destiny, citing a long genealogy and quoting a secret document found in the chest. He says of his ancestors, with varying factual accuracy;

Somerled made many attempts to capture the Merble chair or Stone of destiny of Kennth Macalpin. It was not until 1329 as Bruce lay dying, that John, eldest son of Angus, and his followers brought the stone of Destiny to Skye.

John was crowned Regulus of the Isles in the year 1354. John when he assumed power turned out to be a drunken lout. His drunken orgies . . . brought great displeasure and disgrace on the clan. He was cruel to his little wife Amy, who feared for her life. Most of John's followers having deserted him, helped Amy to escape with their young son Donald whom John was seeking to murder one terrible March night during one of his drunken orgies. They fled to the Monastery of Sadell. Amy's *followers brought the Stone, the Oaken Kist of Somerled, the Golden Circlet, Bracelets and Collar of Somerled.*

John divorced his wife Amy. Donald 2 was brought up in the ways of the Lord. He was anointed and crowned Regulus of the Isles at 12 years old in the years of Grace 1366 by Father John of Sadell. During the Banquet, the golden Collar of an hundred peices of fine gold, was stolen from the sleeping prince while resting in his bedchambder believed by Robert high Steward of Scotland and John . . . never recovered . . . Hear endeth the certified true copy of the origional manuscript written by the mOnks of Sadell now tattered and in peices and almost unreadable . . .

'. . . 'The Stone' known as 'Lia Fail' or Stone of Destiny is this day with the Oaken Kist containing the golden Circlet, Golden Bracelet set with precious stones, removed to a place of great secrecy. known only to the eldest son in direct blood sucession. Hear the secret will be kept even under penalty of death.

'Set by my hand this twenty third day of March in the year of Grace seventeen hundred and twenty. Calean Macdonald. fifteenth prince of the Isles and of Sleat.'

Macdonald included a sketch drawn from memory, of his Stone.

At Register House in Edinburgh experts were intrigued, but thought the lettering and the phraseology suggested that the manuscript was unlikely to be genuine—at least at its date of 1720. Margaret Macdonald, Curator of the Library at the Clan Donald Centre agrees the family tree is faulty. Clearly the letter writer is not connected with the Macdonalds of Sleate, yet he does seem genuinely to have believed he had some claim to a family relic. What motivated him to give this secret away? Why divulge a valuable piece of family information to an individual one doesn't even know? Could he have been trying to get back at a relative who had denied him an

The Stone of Destiny may be hidden in a cave behind a waterfall like this one on Skye.

inheritance, or recognition? Was he perhaps the black sheep of the family? Had he come back from the war warped in some way— a crank? Or is there a flavour of truth in what he wrote? Strenous efforts have been made to trace him over the years, through the good offices of Somerset House, and a variety of newspapers and journals, but all have failed. Did he exist? Was he writing under a pseudonym—and if so, why?

There may be another source of information about Skye and its Stone awaiting study. At the time of the Reformation many documents were sent from Scotland to the Vatican for safe-keeping. They are still there, many of them having already been scrutinised by learned scholars, and they do give valuable information. Dr Norman MacDougall of St Andrews University mentions in his magnificent biography of James 1V (1989) that he did travel to the islands. He does not specify why, but there is a legend that he went in order to have himself properly crowned on the Stone there. Much may remain to be discovered about this.

If there is indeed a Stone on Skye, where might it be hidden? Margaret Macdonald, of the Clan Donald library, suggested a search round *Loch nam Uamh*, the Loch of the Cave, which lies in the hills to the north of Armadale. After a lot of walking and searching however, no cave was to be found, but the terrain is rock and bog, and caves can be blocked with mud especially when assisted by people filling the entrances with boulders. Yet another tradition turned up though, that once, many years ago, there was a secret tunnel from somewhere near Tarskavaig through which you could reach Loch nam Uamh. Possi

bly this was an old mineworking. There are caves on Sleat, particularly on the north-west coast, and in the cliffs to the south-east: a Stone could very easily be hidden in one of these.

And of course there is the other possibility. Whenever a mere lowlander goes looking for something in the Highlands, be it an illicit still or a lost Stone, as we saw in Chapter 2 when the unfortunate Sassenachs were given the runaround by Kay Matheson and her friends, he is liable to be given less than helpful answers to his questions, which are answered by locals with their Gaelic tongues firmly planted in their cheeks, and who are not about to divulge their well-kept secrets to a mere 'foreigner.' The more drams the researcher offers as bribes, the better the laugh the Gaels can have, behind their hands, next day.

There may, then, be a mysterious Stone hiding in a cave on Skye. It may be the case that somebody knows its whereabouts—or it may have been taken into the care of a body of men who have a secret organisation.

Inveraray Castle

18. The Knights Templar

For many centuries, some of the descendants of Angus Og and various other well-connected Scottish families have been members of an organisation known nowadays as the *Ordugh Rioghail Cathachail Teampuill Ierusalem*—the Scottish Knights Templar—who are interested in several ancient Stones. They have recently bought a church for the safe-keeping of one Stone in particular. They are also interested in the whereabouts of the mysterious Arthurian Holy Grail, and amateur historian Archie McKerracher finds reason to believe there may be some connection between the Stone of Destiny and the Holy Grail.

Nine Crusaders founded *The Order of Poor Knights of Christ and the Temple of Solomon* in Jerusalem in 1118 AD, their purpose being to police the pilgrim routes to the Holy Land. King Baudioun I of Jerusalem was so pleased he gave them space in his palace—reputedly built over the ruins of Solomon's Temple—hence their name. Young European nobles rushed to join. Its ideals were Arthurian—oaths of chastity, obedience and poverty were sworn which turned the boys out as military monks, highly skilled fighters in touch with God, obliged to fight to the death. They didn't shave, and wore uniform white surcoats emblazoned with a splayed scarlet cross front and back. Responsible only to the Pope, they became known as the Knights Templar.

People showered them with gifts and privileges, and they arrived in Scotland in 1128, invited by King David I to be 'the custodian of his morals'—and a useful bodyguard.

The Stone features in the records of both the Knights Templar and Scottish Freemasonry. 'The first mention of the Holy Grail in 1130 refers to it not as a cup or chalice but *lapsit exillis*, a stone from heaven' writes McKerracher. Some form of lettering was inscribed around its edge—which makes it comply with early descriptions of the Stone of Destiny. The guardians chosen to care for it were the Knights Templar. Eventually Templars held over 500 Scottish properties, and one of their typical circular churches still exists at The Temple, London.

When the Holy Land fell to the Saracens in 1291 the Knights had to find a new raison d'etre. By 1306 their wildness and power was scaring King Philippe IV, who persuaded Pope Clement V to excommunicate them, and the Order was finished in Europe. McKerracher believes this is why they were in a position to alter the balance of power between Scotland and England in the early 14th century.

Bishop William Lamberton of St Andrews had been ordered by both Edward II of England and the Pope to weed the Templars out of Scotland. But Lamberton remained utterly loyal to the excommunicated Robert the Bruce and to Scot tish independence. McKerracher suggests that, far from interrogating two Templars at Holyrood in December 1309, Lamberton came to an arrangement with them; sanctuary in Scotland in return for arms, money and expertise. Papal Bulls were not being proclaimed in Scotland, therefore the Templars could not legally be dissolved there. They had stockpiles of armaments in Ireland, and shipping to bring them over. Edward II is on record complaining about the import of arms to Scotland at this time.

A group of masons, later known as the 'Loch Awe School', made carvings of remarkable quality dating from the early 1300s—a sword is the

above and opposite Archie McKerracher believes these are Templar grave-slabs, at Kilmartin, Argyll.

unmistakable sign of a Templar's grave. Grave-slabs like those around Kilmartin are unique to Argyll and its islands. The ships depicted are different from west coast galleys of the period. Are they mementoes of the lost Templar fleet?

Sir Iain Bosville Macdonald of Sleat and many others now agree it is highly likely that Bruce was assisted at Bannockburn by the Templars. Studies of contemporary methods of warfare, descriptions of the battle and of Bruce's style of fighting demonstrate Templar strategies and techniques, not seen in Scotland before.

He commanded only about 6000 men, mainly infantry. At a time when foot-soldiers were usually poorly organised, Bruce's army was disciplined and astonishingly well equipped, each man having a leather headpiece and steel helmet, thickly padded leather coat, flexible steel gloves for holding his iron-tipped 12 foot spear, a knife, an axe and a sword. Such weaponry cost far more than Bruce could have scraped from his coffers, with Scotland's economy in ruins, and many of his wealthy lowland nobles believing it would serve their interests better to fight for England. Bruce, desperate for reconciliation with the Pope, daren't record Templar help, and Archdeacon Barbour would have edited out of his epic poem 'The Brus' an order whose name was anathema to his church.

What happened to the Templars in Scotland after that? There is some evidence that the ensuing secret society made a useful information grapevine for Jacobite nobles. Certain Scottish lords are to this day involved in Freemasonry. A Templar Cross was reputedly found on Graham of Claverhouse when he died at Killicrankie.

A mason's set-square and a templar's cross are portrayed on a gravestone at Kilmory, Argyll, demonstrating the link between Templar and Mason. And there are connections with Melrose Abbey too, whose insignia, as we have seen, includes the Rose and the Mell—the mason's hammer. Nowadays the Templars meet at Melrose once a year.

Chaplain of Dundee Preceptory is Chevalier the Reverend John Mackay Nimmo, a keen Scottish Nationalist. Recently the Templars have bought a church in the pretty village of Dull, near Aberfeldy. In it they have installed one Stone which is in their possession, and which they say is the Stone of Destiny recovered from Westminster Abbey in 1950. It was found in Parliament Square in Edinburgh in 1965 and was kept by Revd Nimmo in his church, St Columba's, in Dundee until 1990, where it lay in an iron cage for all to see. The Revd Nimmo affirms the Templars have the real Stone. 'Baillie Gray, a friend of mine, annealed the Stone—put the two parts together . . . We had a mobbed service at the reception of the Stone (in Dundee). My wife said "Come on Baillie, tell us the truth", and he said, "Lassie, do you think I would take part in this kind of a service over a phoney stone? No, no. This is the real Stone of Destiny."'

When St Columba's Church was closed in 1990 the Stone was sent for safe keeping into the charge of Elspeth King, then Curator of the People's Palace Museum in Glasgow. Did it contain bronze dowels—a prerequisite to prove it was the one mended by Gray? As we have seen in Chapter 2, materials testing consultants Harry Stanger Ltd offered to find out. Their tests gave print-outs that told all that needed to be known about what lay hidden inside that Stone. Ian Hamilton came over to the People's Palace from the High Court to keep an eye on things, and the results will be revealed in the final chapter.

Meanwhile a seer, Sweyn Macdonald of Ardgay in Easter Ross who has had the second sight since he was a boy, and who is himself a trained stonemason, recalls a night in the sixties. With speedy, emphatic Highland declamation—like a Knox delivering the Truth—he says: 'You couldn't make a King without a Stone—that was their

belief. The one I saw would be about three-quarters of a hundredweight—a block of grey sandstone about eighteen inches by twelve, four or five inches high. The edges is smooth, no marks, worn like a doorstep, a slight wear in the centre as if it could have been used for stepping on, a little hollow—maybe it was water dripping on it. I was involved with a crowd of Scottish Nationalists in Edinburgh. We *do* need a Parliament in Edinburgh. We were having a discussion and the Stone came up. Two or three days later I was invited to an old ruined place and I was shown the real Stone. They brought it out and let me see it to prove it to me. There's another one that was made to represent it. There's only three people at a time that is allowed to know the ex-

act whereabouts of that Stone—if two were killed there's a third to hand it on. You are the first person that I've ever told—not even my close family— It belongs to a Scottish *organisation*.'

'The Knights Templar?'

'You said that, lass, I didn't. There's another Stone, older than that—I saw two of them. Near Scone Palace. In that area. They brought it out for me—I didn't see the exact place where it was hidden. And I tell you lass it will never be discovered until *until*—we have our Home Rule. The Stone has to remain hidden because I know that if the English got it they'd take it away and *destroy* it.'

At present there are some 150 members of the Scottish Knights Templar, including ministers, headmasters and academics. They possess a secret, alternative, version of Scotland's history, contained in their '*Stella Templum*', and which refers to four Stones: St Columba's Seat, the Pictish Stone, the Celtic Stone, and the Stone of Destiny. They do not tell the public at large where these are kept.

If the Knights Templar exhibit one Stone, where are the other three—do they in fact exist? For no-one so far has been able to describe them. It would be good if one could persuade the Knights to release photographs or drawings of these mysterious objects, in the interests of accuracy and truth. Having such a relatively unbroken link with the legendary past of Scotland, they would seem to be particularly well-placed to inform and to educate the rest of us, especially on the subject of Stones of Destiny. But perhaps what is needed, instead, is a more scientific approach.

below Rev. John Mackay Nimmo and the Knights Templar were forced to move their stone from Dundee when St Columba's Church closed.

PART IV

19. Sir Walter Scott and Edinburgh Castle

As far as the general public were concerned, the Stone languished in Westminster Abbey. Since 1206, monarch after monarch was crowned upon it, first English, then from the seventeeth century British. Any person who might have known of the whereabouts of any alternative Stone was either dead or sworn to very effective secrecy. But it was not forgotten.

Instead, the Stone began to rematerialise, as just a sentence here and there in history books, then as a few paragraphs in the work of a master story-teller. Walter Scott was born in College Wynd, Edinburgh in 1771, at a time when Scottish literature was coming into its own. Educated at Edinburgh High School, he studied law at Edinburgh University, and by the time he was called to the Bar aged twenty-one several writers were putting Scotland on the literary map. At the age of thirty-three Robert Burns was being feted in the capital for his Kilmarnock edition of poems, and Edinburger James Boswell had published his famous Journal.

Before Scott was forty, as we have seen, Jane Porter was writing her 'modern romance' *Scottish Chiefs* (1810). This book, about 'the sister kingdoms', became highly popular— clearly its subject matter struck a chord with readers. It was translated into Russian & German, and brought her fan letters from Moscow to India. Napoleon even denounced it as 'dangerous to the state' and blocked its French publication. Beginning with the murder of Lady Wallace, it follows the fortunes of the Stone, and ends with Bannockburn.

In her preface Porter expresses the feeling of the day: while 'It is now too common to contemn [sic] as nonsense even an honest pride in ancestry . . . Happy it is for this realm that the destiny which now unites the once contending arms of those brave families has also consolidated their rival nations into one, and by planting the heir of Plantagenet and of Bruce upon one throne, hath redeemed the peace of Britains, and fixed it on lasting foundations.'

Happy thought indeed.

A great flowering of science and philosophy was taking place at this time. The bitter pill of Union had been swallowed, General Wade's roads had made the countryside of Scotland accessible—and controllable—the Jacobites had been sent packing and peace reigned. Meanwhile elsewhere, Madame Guillotine was chopping up French aristocrats, in America President George Washington was building his White House, in India Ranjit Singh ruled, Russia was grabbing Black Sea resorts from the Turks and helping itself to Poland, and Austria was being aggressive all over Europe.

Scott was fascinated by Scottish history, and wrote reams about it. In 1805 he published *The*

Edinburgh Castle, from the Grassmarket

Lay Of The Last Minstrel, ten years later *Lord Of The Isles*. During this period he bought and rebuilt his beloved house on the Tweed near Melrose in the Borders and called it Abbotsford.

Scott first enthusiastically recounted his history of Scotland to Johnnie Lockhart, alias 'Hugh Littlejohn Esq', his six year-old grandson, as they rode together under the summer trees by the river. These *Tales of a Grandfather* (1827) are full of warmth and affection. He begins by explaining 'How Scotland and England came to be separate Kingdoms' before their union. By Chapter 6 he has reached the fateful year of 1296.

> Edward marched through Scotland at the head of a powerful army, compelling all ranks of people to submit to him. He removed to London the records of the kingdom of Scotland, and was at pains to transport to the Abbey Church at Westminster a great stone, upon which it had been the national custom to place the King of Scotland when he was crowned for the first time. He did this to show that he was absolute master of Scotland, and that the country was in future to have no other king but himself, and his descendants the Kings of England. The stone is still preserved, and to this day the King's throne is placed upon it at the time when he is crowned. Last of all, King Edward placed the government of Scotland in the hands of John de Warenne, earl of Surrey . . . He placed English soldiers in all the castles and strongholds of Scotland, from the one end of the kindgom to the other; and not trusting the Scots themselves, he appointed English governors in most of the provinces of the kingdom . . . Perhaps Edward thought to himself that, by uniting the whole island of Britain under one king and one government, he would do so much good

by preventing future wars, as might be an excuse for the force and fraud which he made use of to bring about his purpose. But, my dear child . . . We must not do evil even that good may come of it; and the happy prospect that England and Scotland would be united under one government, was so far from being brought nearer by Edward's unprincipalled usurpation, that the hatred and violence of national antipathy which arose betwixt the sister countries, removed to a distance almost incalculable, the prospect of their becoming one people, for which nature seemed to design them.

Scott adds a footnote:

'This fatal stone was said to have been brought from Ireland by Fergus, the son of Eric, who led the Dalriads to the shores of Argyleshire. Its virtues are preserved in the celebrated leonine verse 'Ni fallat fatum[etc]. . . ' which may be rendered thus:-

Unless the fates are faithless found,
And prophets' voice be vain,
Where'er this monument is found
The Scottish race shall reign.'

'There were Scots who hailed the accomplishment of this prophecy at the accession of James V1 to the crown of England, and exulted, that in removing this palladium, the policy of Edward resembled that which brought the Trojan horse in triumph within their walls, and which occasioned the destruction of their royal family.'

In fact, while Edward I stayed in the Castle in 14th June 1296—before he went to Scone, he forced his way into the royal treasuries of Scotland. There, as we saw in Chapters 13 to 15, he selected such things as he thought proper to be removed as *spolia opima* (spoils of war), partly to enrich his own treasury and partly, as with Wales, to remove the central nervous system of the body that was Scotland—to break the Scottish spirit. He removed or destoyed the kingdom's ancient records. These are shown in an inventory, *Inventa in Castro de Edeneburgh* along with those he had taken a few years before

Sir Walter Scott so loved Melrose Abbey that he helped himself to several cartloads of its ancient stones to build into his house, Abbotsford.

at Norham. He also took the Crown and Sceptre and the other insignia of sovereignty.

On his way south from Scone, Edward arrived back in Edinburgh on Friday 17 August 1296. One account details that he 'sent three chests of the royal records to London, so much as could be found of the royal plate, the Black Rood of his ancestress St Margaret, and the crowning stone that Fergus, first king of Dalriada, had brought from Ireland'.

But Margaret Harrison, Principal Librarian at Jordanhill College, Glasgow, recalls reading somewhere 'about the discovery of an unusual stone during the renovation of Edinburgh Castle at the beginning of the 19th century. Sir Walter Scott and other antiquaries were called in to examine the stone and the author speculated that this might have been the original Stone of Destiny'. Some say he positively identified this.'

His writings show that, being a balanced sort of a person and no Nationalist, Scott was not above having a healthy laugh at the expense of his compatriots from time to time. He was a known practical joker, and found opportunities for mischief quite irresistible. On one occasion he published a paper on a 'prehistoric rock carving' near Yarrow for the Proceedings of the Society of Antiquaries of Scotland, only recently debunked in that august publication by rock expert Ronald Morris.

Could the Stone still lie hidden in Edinburgh Castle? It is possible that the real one did arrive there from Scone, but that in the ten days or so that elapsed between its removal from Scone and Edward's return to Edinburgh or between then and its despatch southward, some enterprising soul swapped it for the fake that went to Westminster—in which case the original may be there yet, hidden in some undiscovered dungeon.

On Scott's own way into history, he influenced many people, not least Queen Victoria, who created her Highland home at Balmoral and made Scotland fashionable. He also encouraged his fellow-writers, with generosity and foresight. In 1813 Scott refused a proffered Laureateship for himself and recommended Southey. He died aged sixty-one, having discovered James Hogg, the 'Ettrick Shepherd' (1770-1835) who had helped him with material for his *Border Minstrelsy*. Scott's success encouraged a variety of Scottish enterprises. The Gaelic-speaking son of a Kingussie farmer, James Macpherson (1736-96), 'translated' Ossian's poetry to acclaim from Goethe and challenge from Dr Johnson, but was popular enough to be buried in Westminster Abbey. William Blackwood thought it worthwhile to start a magazine in 1817, and in 1882 the Scottish Text Society was founded, which then began to publish rare manuscripts such as Barbour's *The Brus*. Scott may not have found the Stone of Destiny itself, but he was responsible for keeping an interest alive in Scottish history, myth and legend, and as a result much has survived in popular culture that would otherwise have withered and died for lack of love.

It was in Scott's lifetime that an interesting Stone was dug up in Perthshire.

20. Macbeth's Castle

Early in the nineteenth century, on New Year's day 1819, at a time when Scott was engendering an interest in history, when amateur archaeology was beginning to become popular, and when writers and poets were taking a new interest in myth and legend, the *Times* published a letter from Dunsinan in Scotland, entitled 'Macbeth's Castle—Curious Discovery'. It stated as follows:

> *On the 19th November, as the servants belonging to the West Mains of Dunsinane house, were employed in carrying away stones from the excavation made among the ruins that point out the site of Macbeth's Castle here, part of the ground they stood on suddenly gave way, and sunk down about six feet, discovering a regularly built vault, about six feet long and four wide. None of the men being injured, curiosity induced them to clear out the subterranean recess, when they discovered among the ruins a large stone, weighing about 500 l, which is pronounced to be of the meteoric or semi-metallic kind. This stone must have lain here during the long series of ages since Macbeth's reign.*
>
> *Besides it were also found two round tablets, of a composition resembling bronze. On one of these two lines are engraved, which a gentleman has thus deciphered—"The sconce (or shadow) of kingdom come, until sylphs in air carry me again to Bethel." These plates exhibit the figures of targets for the arms.*

> *'From time immemorial it has been believed among us here, that unseen hands brought Jacob's pillow from Bethel, and dropped it on the site where the palace of Scoon now stands. A strong belief is also entertained by many in this part of the country, that it was only a representation of this Jacob's pillow that Edward sent to Westminster, the sacred stone not having been found by him. The curious here, aware of such traditions, and who have viewed these venerable remains of antiquity, agree that Macbeth may, or rather must, have deposited the stone in question at the bottom of his Castle, on the hill of Dunsinane (from the trouble of the times), where it has been found by the work-men . . .*

On the following day the same letter appeared in the *Morning Chronicle*, and throughout January it was to appear in several other English and Scottish newspapers, such as the *Edinburgh Evening Chronicle*, the *Glasgow Herald*, and the *Caledonian Mercury*. The letter is, in every case, unattributed. Is its credibility therefore in doubt? Could it have been a Ne'erday hoax? One has to admit that possibility. And yet—does the ring of truth not echo down the ages, 'from time immemorial it has been believed among us here . . .'? There is an earlier source of the tradition. Seton Gordon quotes a story passed down through the Earls of Mansefield, hereditary owners of Scone Palace:

Somewhere around the dates 1795-1820, a farm lad had been wandering with a friend on Dunsinnan . . . soon after a violent storm. The torrential rain had caused a small landslide, and as the result of this a fissure, which seemed to penetrate deep into the hillside was visible. The two men procured some form of light and explored the fissure. They came at last to the broken wall of a subterranean chamber. In one corner of the chamber was a stair which was blocked with debris, and in the centre of the chamber they saw a slab of stone covered with hieroglyphics and supported by four short stone legs. As there was no evidence of 'treasure' in the subterranean apartment the two men did not realise the importance of their find and did not talk of what they had seen.

Some years later one of the men first heard the local tradition that on the approach of King Edward 1 the monks of Scone hurriedly removed the Stone of Destiny to a place of safe concealment and took from the Annety Burn a stone of similar size and shape, which the English king carried off in triumph. When he heard this legend the man hurried back to Dunsinnan Hill, but whether his memory was at fault regarding the site of the landslide, or whether the passage of time, or a fresh slide of earth, had obliterated the cavity, the fact remains that he was unable to locate the opening in the hillside.

Seton Gordon discusses the question of why the 13th century monks of Scone had not returned the Stone to the Abbey after Edward had gone:

the tradition accounts for this by explaining that it was not considered safe at the time to allow the English to know that they had been tricked, and that when the days of possible rebribution were past the monks who had known the secret were dead.

In 1819, in spite of the famous Enlightenment, ordinary Scots were a cowed people, some being cleared off the land in favour of sheep, then being exported by the boat-load to the colonies, others seeking their fortunes in India— newly colonised into the British Empire, to become yet another area to be printed in pink on the world map, pink denoting so-called British territory. London was perceived as the epicentre of government, of manners and of speech.

But the old story-telling tradition was still very much a part of everyday life at all levels of society, and not only in Scotland. The Perthshire legend of Dunsinnan was clearly well-known locally and, like others of its kind, is likely therefore to have contained at least a grain of truth.

Why was the letter not attributed in any of the papers? Because it was considered vulgar for writers to publicise their names. Even famous novelists like Scott and Dickens would serialise their work anonymously.

Was the *Times* letter written by a group of jokers? This seems unlikely, because the personality of an individual shines through, the tone neither pompous nor facetious, the writer clearly feeling that the servants not being injured was worthy of report. He knew something of Scottish history, but the inaccuracy about MacBeth shows this knowledge was faulty, so perhaps the writer was not an academic, though the language is that of a reasonably well-educated person. He reports what the servants experienced—not that he himself witnessed the event described. His attitude is dated, too, showing no idea of archaeological stratification, whereby sites are layered according to successive waves of occupation—he presupposed that all the finds were laid down at one time. The fact that so many newspaper editors gave the letter space that January shows that they believed the entire reading population of Britain would be interested in its contents.

For some unstated reason, that year Dr James

Playfair, Principal of St Andrews University, suddenly undertook an excavation of Macbeth's Castle on Dunsinnan Hill, which lies, as he wrote, ' in the Sidla ridge, 7 miles SSW of Cupar . . . of a conical form, 1024 feet above the level of the sea.'

His report is almost exactly the wording of the anonymous entry in the Statistical Account which it is generally accepted was also written by him:

Its summit is an oval area 210 feet from east to west, and 130 feet in breadth; which M. fortified with a strong rampart of stone, cemented with red mortar. Penetrating horizontally seven yards into the ruins of this rampart, I lately discovered a part of it as entire as when it was originally constructed. Founded with rock, it is neatly built of large stones. If the rubbish on the outside were removed this would be one of the most remarkable monuments of antiquity in Britain. At the foot of that wall there was a level walk of considerable breadth, and 231 yards in circuit, secured by a parapet and ditch. Having diligently explored the area of the fortress, now 3 feet below the surface, and cut a deep trench across it, I found no vestige of buildings in it; so the temporary houses were probably composed of wood. In one corner great quantities of charcoal, bones of black cattle, sheep and hares were dug up, but none of the human body. From the summit of this hill, there is a delightful prospect of Strathmore, the Lomond hills, Birnam Hill and part of Strathearn. The fortress was demolished in the year 1057.

This was the first of several archaeological digs on Dunsinnan Hill. Each one was to find a little more evidence than the other, and each left a trail of wreckage in its wake.

The letter-writer's inexactitude about MacBeth's dates —he reigned in the 11th century—gave two people food for creative thought. Ten years after its publication, Robert Chambers is enjoying the thought that Shakespeare himself had visited this place, 'and thus became personally acquainted with the localities of the tragedy which he afterwards wrote upon the story of Macbeth' and that therefore 'the traveller will consider Dunsinnan as holy ground'. Chambers makes a point about the ruined rampart 'the height of which is conjectured to have been considerable, from the immense mass remaining'—agreed upon by archaeologists today— and goes on to discuss 'Mr Nairne of Dunsinnan' and his findings: 'A theory has been started, in consequence of Mr Nairne's discovery, that Macbeth, from an implicit faith in the sacred character of the stone, and that the possession of it would insure the continuance of his sovereignty, transferred it to a close concealment in his fortress, subsiting in its place a similar stone, which has ever since been accepted as the real one.' According to Chambers then, no less than twelve Scottish Kings would have been crowned on MacBeth's replacement stone at Scone before Edward I got it.

The second writer describes Nairne's dig and agrees 'It has been supposed that Macbeth may, or rather must have deposited the real Simon Pure (meaning the original Stone of Destiny) in the foundations of his castle, as he would deem its possession of great importance, as a supernatural aid to keep him on his usurped throne, and that to prevent it being purloined he buried it in the foundations of his castle, where it was found in 1818. All this is pleasing and fanciful; but assuming it to be true, we must conclude that Macbeth on removing it from its original site, had substituted another one resembling it in its stead, and this one would be the stone carried off by Edward 1 to Westminster Abbey. 'It is a pity that Mr Nairne did not get the inscription engraved and published, as it is very likely the translation given is incorrect.'

By 1850 James Myles is waxing lyrical about Macbeth's exploits on Dunsinnan Hill, and showing continued interest in the Stone, relating the Nairne story almost verbatim from previous accounts. Five years later a paper is read, at the April meeting of the Society of Antiquaries of Scotland, in which Nairne's excavations and several findings are reported, and a diagram shown of the structure of the ruins on top of the hill. In 1857 the Society reports:

> Upon digging, last year, into the south-east side of the top of the hill, and several feet under the grass covering, four rude chambers were found built of freestone, generally of old red sandstone, some of the varieties of which seem to have been brought from a considerable distance. The stones were all undressed, and carefully built . . . On examining these chambers more carefully, they were found to occupy a quadrangular space and to communicate with each other by small passages, two feet broad, by three in height . . . The southern wall . . . was nearly straight, and was probably the outer wall stated by Principal Playfair to be 5 or 6 feet in height . . . This wall extended backward . . . forming two chambers 20 feet in length, having two entrances . . . These chambers had usually a rounded figure, were

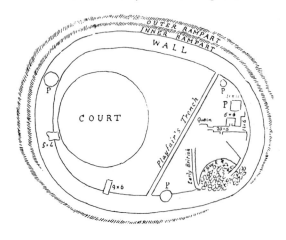

Dunsinann
(The late Mr A Stewart)

7 or 8 feet in diameter; and after the wall had been raised 2 or 3 feet above the stone flooring of the chamber, the stones overlapped each other as the building advanced upwards, so as to form a roof, which was completed by a large flat stone placed over the top, the rude substitute for an arch. The greatest height of these chambers was 6 feet from the floor, which was laid with undressed flags. As the roofs of these chambers had fallen in, or their walls had been disturbed by former excavations, it was not always easy to discover their original figures, particularly as they were filled with black earth and stones, the accumulation of ages . . . the passage . . . between the inner chambers . . . was built up, and on opening it three skulls were found with a number of fragments of human bones.'
The bodies had been placed in a sitting position, with the knees pushed up to the chin. They were 'a 60 year-old woman, an adult male, an adult female and a young child, a female apparently murdered.

In 1871 the Revd Thomas Brown, Minister of Collace, is reporting T. M. Nairne's find, while a trench was being dug near the gateway of the fort, 'lying on the surface of the earth and rubbish which had been thrown up while the digging was going on,' of a small spiral bronze ring in the form of a serpent 'the eyes and scales on the back being carved in the most minute manner . . . it was only when they were looked at through a microscope that their beauty and exquisite workmanship became apparent.' This shows that at least one of the people who fled up to Macbeth's Castle for safety, or who used it for aggression, appreciated art, craft and beautiful things. Sadly it also demonstrates the state of archaelogical understanding at the time, as workmen spaded out 'rubbish'. The carelessness of the day is also in evidence. The ring was given to Mr Nairne, who managed to lose it after only a year.

A doorway was discovered, 'consisting of two

Macbeth's Castle is an ancient fort at the top of Dunsinann Hill in Perthshire.

rude unhewn slabs forming the posts, and a similar slab forming the lintel. From the doorway, which was low and narrow, and could not have been entered by a man in an upright position, there was a sloping passage leading to what seemed to be a house or burrow of considerable size, but underground; so that, while the house, if such it can be called would have contained more than one, perhaps two or three persons, the doorway could only have admitted one at a time, and the passage could easily have been defended by any one armed with a spear.'

Again, there is no actual mention of a Stone. But there's plenty of evidence that the Nairne family, who owned the land including Dunsinane Hill, were searching the area—and that chambers or buildings were indeed hidden beneath its turfs. With such clear motivation to carry on digging on the part of the landowner, and if so much of the farm labourers' tale is true, why would the rest of it be false? Why, then, have no academic papers so far discovered mentioned the Stone? To begin with Archaeology was a hobby for amateur historians, but those interested wanted to make it into an academic discipline in its own right. It therefore had to be developed along serious and scientific lines, in which idle speculation could not be allowed. Archaeologists then and now dare not risk their reputations by putting down in print romantic nonsense about disappearing rocks.

Yet, for some reason, Victorian antiquarians continued to turn the site over. What had aroused their curiousity? The state of their art was so crude that they ruined the site for further research, so that only those in the forefront of archaeology would be able to learn anything new there today.

The sheer number of digs undertaken shows Dunsinnan was attracting far greater interest than a small hill-fort would normally have merited, at a time when sites of major significance such as Scone and Forteviot were still un-touched—indeed are still unexplored.

Who were these Nairnes? These custodians of Dunsinnan Hill were guilty of quite some prodigality. They managed to lose not only the little ring, but also the unearthed Stone, after it has been safely hidden for centuries, so successfully that no trace of it remains. Their loss is symptomatic of their lack of regard for the artefacts of Scotland. The Nairne family sold the Estate in 1898 and scattered themselves between Africa and America. For a time Dunsinnan House belonged to the Bernard family, Edinburgh brewers, and now it is the property of Jamie Sinclair who says of the Stone 'we like to think it is still hidden on the hill!'.

Journalist Margaret Wilson has long been fascinated by the Dunsinnan story and has worked for years, trying to trace Nairne descendants because, she says, there must be papers, letters and records in existence of the activities of such an important Scottish family. In these, wherever they are, may lie further clues as to the present resting place of the Dunsinnan Stone.

Meanwhile there has been controversy over the hill because a quarry at its base is threatening to gobble it up. The National Trust and other bodies have performed a holding operation whereby Macbeth's castle cannot be touched without their consent.

Ann and Peter Campbell are tenant farmers whose sheep roam Dunsinnan Hill. Ann writes that they have 'always known the real stone of Destiny is hidden in a cave on the hill. The Monks of Scone Abbey are said to have put it there and gave King Edward I a replica . . . A few years ago I read in the *Dundee Courier* that a gamekeeper was on the hill one day when there was a small landslide and he discovered a cave. Inside the cave he claims to have seen the 'Stone', by the time he went and got the laird and

a few others another landslide had occurred and the cave had vanished'

The letter to *The Times* ended, tantalisingly, ' . . . *This curious stone has been shipped to London for the inspection of the scientific amateur, in order to discover its real quality.*' So did the Stone, after all, end up in London?

A search was carried out in London during 1990 and it was learned that between 1817-1823 the Society of Antiquaries of London was the recipient of most newly discovered artefacts. Its members came from a wide variety of backgrounds, and the President, who chaired most of the meetings, happened to be a Scotsman, the Earl of Aberdeen. Many archaeological finds were discussed, occasionally of Scottish origin, but the Proceedings mention no large Stone, from Scotland or anywhere else. A search at the British Museum, repository of all earlier and smaller collections, with the help of Sue Youngs, Curator of Medieval and Later Antiquities, revealed nothing.

If the Stone was 'shipped' it would be listed. The cargoes of all the ships arriving in the Thames were faithfully reported in the newspapers of the day. A careful scrutiny of these over a period of a year showed many cargoes arriving from Scotland, in ships which had suffered an interesting variety of accidents. No cargo included a Stone. This tallies with research done by McKerracher in Scotland, who checked reports of all ships sailing out of Perth over that period and found them empty of sizeable stones. Although 'shipped' might be considered a loose term also applied to the moving of freight on dry land, at that time Perth and the Tay, which is still navigable by sea-going boats, were by far the most feasible options for shipment of large and heavy objects. Unless and until further research shows otherwise, we can now be reasonably certain that wherever the Dunsinnan Stone went after mid-December 1818, it did not leave Scotland. It may yet, therefore, turn up in Perthshire.

There are a few more tantalising shreds of information. Lady Pamela Mansefield remembers hearing her father-in-law the late Lord Mansefield say the Stone had been 'carted away' from the site 'in the 1920s'. And D. M. Heyde, who once attempted to find the entrance to Dunsinnan fort cites a local tradition that the Stone was taken 'in the first instance' to Bandirran, near Balbeggie—the village nearest to Dunsinnan Hill—though 'its subsequent disposal remains a mystery.'

In 1927 Dundee archaeologist Alexander Hutcheson, who seems to have got into the chamber on the hill himself in 1870, wrote that when Nairne's men discovered the underground chamber and the stone, they brought it down and carted it away. He mentioned the two plaques and their inscription, giving his opinion that, while the place-name Bethel was not in doubt, the rest of the translation was probably not very good. McKerracher reasons that the Dunsinnan Stone is the real Stone of Destiny. He asks why, when Edward I had ordered Master Adam the Goldsmith to encase the Stone he had looted in a bronze chair, he cancelled it when it was only half-completed. Why had he then suddenly sent a raiding party of knights back to Scone on 17th August, 1298, who, according to the Chartulary of Scone, ripped the Abbey apart in a desperate search for something. They returned empty-handed. A furious Edward ordered Walter the painter to make a wooden chair for the stone at a cost of a hundred shillings. He declared this was no longer to be for the use of the monarch regnant, but 'for the use of the priest celebrant'.

McKerracher goes on: 'The preliminary negotiations for the Treaty of Northampton in 1328 . . . included the offer of the return of the Stone. Strangely, the Scots did not ask for the insertion of this clause in the formal document. Edward 111 offered to return it in 1328 and again in 1329, even suggesting the Queen Mother would take it personally to Berwick. It was offered a final time in 1363, but on none of these occasions do the Scots appear to have replied. So the sandstone block in London stayed where it was, and the real Stone . . . was almost certainly hidden by Abbot Henry . . . and as only a few senior monks would have known the location, it is likely this became lost through the passage of time. The Scots knew it was still within Scotland and thus made no effort to have the fake returned from London'.

McKerracher would like to find the plaques, reminding us that the Great Seals of Malcolm V, Alexander 1, and David 1 show the Stone of Destiny flanked on either side 'by two round plaques, or targes, which bear armorial insignia'. He says the inscription 'deciphered' by 'a gentleman' does hold a clue in the words 'sconce (or shadow)' that 'the inscription was in Gaelic, for the meaning of sconce in that language is a protective shadow. A Gaelic scholar put the sentence back into that language and then re-translated it, and what came out was 'Under your protective shadow lies the kingdom until angels carry you back to Bethel' . . .

Acair's 1989 Gaelic dictionary gives *faileas* for 'shadow' and *tearmunnach* for 'protective'. *Sgonnsa* is unequivocally given as 'fort'. Over the centuries, in every language, words change meaning and connotation—perhaps the early Gaelic of mid-Perthshire mutated?

But McKerracher is 'now convinced that this was the real Stone of Scone, and that this was the saying connected with it of which a vague memory had been handed down.'

21. A Royal Peculiar

For most people, however, the Stone which Edward 1 had taken so long ago to Westminster Abbey was always regarded as the one and only Stone of Destiny. By early in the twentieth century, as we saw in Part 1, a few individuals were beginning to think in terms of making a political gesture by bringing it back to Scotland, and in 1950 Hamilton, Matheson et al had succeeded in achieving this aim.

They and their sympathisers clearly thought the Westminster Stone belonged to the Scottish people, and they had good reason to believe this, because treaty after treaty with England since 1296 had promised its return.

But, even after Westminster got a stone back that April day in 1951, the question was not resolved. For some reason charges were not pressed. No prosecutions took place and the young reivers were not brought to 'justice'. No satisfactory explanations were ever given to the public about the reasons for this waiving of the normal formalities. The trouble was that unless ownership could be proved, Westminster would have had no case.

Meanwhile King George VI died and his elder daughter Elizabeth was crowned Queen, over whatever stone lay beneath the Coronation Chair, according to the English tradition described in Chapter 1, as had her forebears since the Union of Crowns in 1603, which meant that some of the fundamentals of the Scottish ceremony were left to be dealt with ad hoc, or omitted. Wendy Wood, a passionate and irreverent Scottish Nationalist, explained: 'The tradition of royalty in Scotland is different . . . Our kings were much closer to the people as is the Scandinavian royalty today. The King of Scots was once the actual representative of the poor people by whom he could be approached at any time. James IV was the first Trade Unionist in that he worked incognito in the fields and after receiving his wage, sent word that in future payment must be higher. This is our natural tradition of royalty.'

When, therefore, it was announced that the Queen was to be known as Elizabeth II, many Scots objected, including Wood. While the Coronation was going on at Westminster she was declaring to the public in Aberdeen 'As you cannot have a second before a first (or there would be more claims for family allowances),' Scotland is henceforth a Republic.'

The Queen came on a State visit to Edinburgh in 1953. She was to receive the Scottish Crown in St Giles Cathedral, Edinburgh. Wood details this event:

> It was 131 years since The Honours of Scotland had been seen outside the walls of Edinburgh Castle, and the capital of Scotland was thrilled. But the occasion was obviously

to be played down by the authorities from London. Court instruction implied that the peers were not expected to wear their robes . . . but to Scotland this was equivalent to the coronation in London.

They went ahead and wore the lot. Journalists described how 'Walter Elliot gleamed in the gold lace of a Privy Councillor. The bonnet feathers and bows of the Royal Archers, the peers in scarlet and ermine, the Countess of Errol in her crimson robe, all was splendid and full of colour . . . But the Queen? She was in a plain blue shopping dress; it seemed like a slap in the face for the nation. The very Revd Charles Warr, who received Her Majesty at the door, looked as if he were going to faint from shock . . . At the great moment in St Giles when the Duke of Hamilton presented Scotland's Crown to Her Majesty, the Queen stretched out her hand with her bag dangling from her arm! It seemed like a deliberate insult to Scotland and the offending object had to be painted over in the official recording of the event.

Wood was further stunned when, 'On her visit to New Zealand where she styled herself on theadio as "Queen of England", the Maoris were honoured with the real coronation robe.' Gleefully she noted that this blunder gave rise to a court case in which two Scottish sisters refused to pay their income tax to the English Treasury on the legal premise that Her Majesty's reference to herself on a world-wide broadcast as the 'Queen of England' presupposed two different kingdoms and they were only prepared to pay their tax to the Scottish one.

So disgusted was Wood with the insensitive behaviour of the English Court that every pinprick became unbearable. When, in 1962, King Olaf of Norway came to visit Edinburgh, an EIIR sign was reported on the North Bridge.

'The sign was on a shield about twenty-five feet up on a lamp post—a puzzle to get at. It could not at that height be painted out or removed. So I blew three eggs, filled them with waterproof ink, coloured purple, red and black, plugged the holes with plasticine and going to the bridge in the evening, hurled the first egg at the target. It skiffed the side of the board and dived into the street below, with what possible result I shuddered to think. The second egg and the third hit the target, and I felt that having played cricket at school had not been wasted after all. I was on my way home when a reluctant policeman invited me into his box . . . Denial was useless with hands so stained that all the detergents of Leverhulme would not cleanse them.'

In some countries she would have thrown a bomb and started a civil war. Perhaps the Scots' use of irony, and their fondness for defusing situations with ridicule, are rather useful traits.

Yet the frustration continues. Who legally owns the stone at present in Westminster? Does it belong to the Crown, the State, the Church—and if the church, which church? The question of ownership has been argued off and on since the time of Edward I. Because he offered it to St Edward when he got it to Westminster, the Abbotts regarded it as the property of the saint and hence the Church, but the presence of leopards in the decoration of the Coronation Chair shows he regarded the Stone as royal property. So when it was due to be handed back to the Scots in 1328, the throne and the church had a difference of opinion. The *Chronicle of Lanercost* says the abbot refused to let it go, and the Londoners, who saw it as a legitimate trophy of war symbolising the overthrow of the Scottish kingdom, agreed with him. Nowadays the answer must lie somewhere in the convoluted principles of English and Scots law which, as we have seen, differ fundamentally from each other. In fact, ownership of the stone has never yet been established, in spite of the valiant efforts of several Scots to bring a test case before the courts.

What if an original Stone of Destiny should be found in Scotland? Would Scots in any sense 'owe' it to Westminster? Would Scotland Yard come and snatch it away—or would it belong where it was found? And if, as seems quite likely, the Stone presently at Westminster has never been used in a Scottish king-making ceremony, was never the pillow of either St Columba or Jacob, what claim can the Scots possibly have on it? That, having been dug from a Perthshire quarry, it is a piece of absentee land? If Edward's Stone was replaced by a Bertie Gray facsimile in 1951, does it not legally belong to his estate? It might make him a fitting tombstone.

These questions can only be discussed thoroughly in a court of law, but this has never been attempted. Could it be that the complexities of establishing ownership of the Westminster stone are beyond the greatest legal brains in England? Is this why the actions of the English authorities, in both 1296 and 1951, were to grab the Stone, secure it, and only then promise discussion, someday—possession being nine-tenths of the law?

For, although apparently it is only after an attempted theft that ownership requires to be proved, the 1951 conspirators were found and questioned -- and Hamilton has confessed all in his books -- no charges were laid.

It was in an attempt to force open discussion on the ownership question that David Stewart, a twenty-four year-old English-born Scotsman, decided to make his own bid for the Stone in August 1974. Talking fast and emphatically, Stewart explains how, from an early age he had been 'very heavily into politics'. A General Election was due and he wanted to keep the question of Nationalism in the front of people's minds. 'It's always been very difficult to get the Scottish people moving.'

He laid his plans. When he arrived at Westminster Abbey luck appeared to be with him—renovation was going on and all the steps were ramped—the builders themselves had been moving huge stones around. The Coronation Chair was surrounded by spiked railings, apparently of wrought iron—and there was no gate. How could he get in? Using logic—it was clean, therefore cleaners got in, therefore there was a secret opening—and with his minute observation—he was a trained geologist-archaeologist—he noticed a loose spike. 'You can lift it off, and then push the railings in. There's no alarm on the railings'. He worked out how the seat came apart.

He went home to Wolverhampton, made a collapsible trolley, a harness, a ramp for his mini, and packed the pieces into two large shopping bags.

The Abbey opened late on Wednesdays. The car park for the Houses of Parliament was open all night just across the road. 'Things were conspiring in my favour, quite honestly, so I felt pressurised to *do* it'. On the night of 4th September 1974 he drove south.

He had two plans; either to get the Stone away north to Scotland, or, if he should be caught, to be brought to court accused of theft. Either way ownership would have to be tried.

The IRA then 'decided to blow up the Houses of Parliament. They planted a bomb in the cafeteria. So the place was absolutely solid with guards.'

But Stewart decided to go ahead. Held up by traffic, he was late getting into the Abbey. Wandering casually in amongst the last visitors, 'the cable around my body, two enormous carrier bags, and a camera round my neck to look like a tourist,' he suddenly realised he had left his tools in the car.

'I thought—it can't be done. But I've written a letter to the press telling them about this. It's got to be done.' He retrieved them at the run, and re-entered the Abbey just as people were being ushered out. He stopped a guard . 'And because his job was to show people where things were he pointed the way. There's this instinctive behaviour— the fact that one had let you in meant that all the others let you in. They're just people who work late and want to get home.' He hid under an altar till the Abbey shut at eight o'clock. A guard walked round. An hour and a half later came another. 'And that was it. The place was my own.

'I was going to wait till 2 a.m., but I got so bored. I got inside the railings, saw four pressure alarms underneath each corner. If you moved the Stone at all you would set it off. Sometimes you've just got to take a chance. I thought—the alarm may not actually work. There was this gigantic thick five-core wire. I cut through it. Nothing happened.'

He dismantled the Chair and strung his cable to the railings. Tipping the Chair forward he let the Stone fall into the sling. 'It went down with one hell of a crash— just missed my legs. I hadn't realised just how big it was. That was when I found out the railings were *not* wrought iron— they were *cast* iron. One of these big pineapple jobs with the cord round it snapped, whistled over my head at the speed of light and thumped into the tomb of Edward the Confessor. The Stone dropped slam onto the trolley and flattened the front wheels splat. The noise was like the crack of doom—the whole Abbey reverberated. But no-one came.

'I was getting it out, when I heard the police sirens. It's the strangest feeling when you know they're coming for *you*.

'Three or four minutes after, the doors opened and the lights came on. They'd never been in the place in their lives—they didn't know where the Stone was. Somebody turned up eventually, flashed his torch on me—then went away again.

David Stewart decided to make his own bid for the Stone in 1974.

A minute later they turned up in force and that was that.

'They wanted to know where all my mates were. It takes six to move the Stone.

'I was heaved into Brixton prison for a week. Very educational. I'd recommend it to anyone. Very bizarre place. I was charged with theft immediately.

They give you a copy of the charge-sheet. I

was charged with attempting to steal a Stone which was the property of the Dean and Chapter of Westminster.

'Somebody must have realised what the charge implied. I was out doing the rounds of the exercise yard, and someone went through my clothes where the charge sheet was, and took it. Twenty minutes before I was due to appear in Court they told me the charge of theft was dropped.'

Six weeks later, after the General Election, on 22nd October 1974 at Bow Street, Magistrate Evelyn Russell conditionally discharged him, ordering him to pay £150 damages, and £75 costs. A police witness reported that on being apprehended Stewart had said, 'How can I steal something that is already stolen?'

How did he feel? 'Relieved. I'm not a violent man. It was a symbolic gesture. But I had had a damn good look at the Stone. I have to say I never saw a repair on it.'

Stewart confirms that it would be impossible to make a repair which would be undetectable under close inspection although, 'having glued and rivetted the thing together, you could grind up a stone of a similar type, fill the crack, and smear it over. But rings are stuck into the Stone with a lead surround. The refining of lead was only perfected about 1800. Prior to that lead tended to be full of silver. If it's silver-free these rings were replaced post 1800. If there's no record of repair and it's modern lead then you can say categorically it's a forgery.'

If there is no evidence of a repaired crack on the stone at present in Westminster, then it cannot be the one which was taken in 1950, because we know it was repaired with brass dowels and cemented together.

In 1977 Stewart stood for Newington Council in Edinburgh. Having invested twelve years in the SNP, he wanted to stay in Scottish politics, but felt that 'the party's vision stopped the day after Independence—they had no vision.' For him 'The 1979 Referendum was a knife in the heart. It demoralised everybody. If the Scots weren't interested then I felt I wasn't prepared to keep bashing my head against a brick wall indefinitely. So I left and just got on with my job.' He now works as a respectable on-site archaeologist for the Scottish Office, sometimes with Dr Caldwell of the Finlaggan Trust. 'Almost certainly the real Stone of Destiny never went south. Because as David Caldwell says—and he's a man who knows his history of Scotland—the Scots never *asked* for it back. And this was one of their most precious things, their Kingship Stone. So it cannot have been the real one. I'm convinced it's around. But I don't think anyone's keeping it. Because, if they were, they would have used the opportunity sometime in the recent past of saying 'we've got the real one. I keep looking for it. I go digging sites all over Scotland—all archaeologists keep a weather eye out for it, but they're reticent —everyone's looking after their reputations. This is political, and they will take no risks.

'Someone's going to turn it up. It's got to be here. It will be recognisable—it's an important stone and it will have been worked—it's a really scabby piece of garbage, a random block, which is down there in Westminster. '

What if Stewart, or anyone else, should dig up the Stone of Destiny somewhere in Scotland? Legally, all ancient objects discovered in Scotland, whether or not they have intrinsic value, belong first to the Crown. You receive its market value, and possibly that of any treasure trove subsequently found on the site, and your find may be returned to you. In this way the accidental finder can't lose.

Of course one of the problems is recognition that you've found something of special interest. Nowadays we view with horror the builders of Arthurstone House in Perthshire who, two hundred years ago, blew up Arthur's Stone for building materials. But could the farmer in upper Clydesdale who recently bulldozed away the centre of the ancient motte near his farm-steading, for a handy silage pit, be blamed? In Scots law, ignorance is not regarded as an excuse.

At present, says an eminent Scottish QC working in London, there remains the question of whether ownership would be settled by English or Scots law. In England, unless anyone can prove a contrary title, ownership is vested in the Crown.

In 1991 Richard Mortimer, Archivist at Westminster Abbey, kindly replied to an enquiry. 'Experience suggests that the Church rarely speaks with a single voice', but, 'it seems clear that its significance is monarchic rather than religious . . . The Stone legally belongs to the Dean and Chapter of Westminster. The Abbey is a "Royal Peculiar" and comes directly under the Queen, on whose behalf the Dean and Chapter administer the Abbey'.

Who are we to argue with such a statement? We may be the defrauded owners of an ancient relic—or Westminster may be the deluded owners of a graveyard block. Meanwhile amateur Stone-seekers are free to look for alternative pieces of rock art around the bogs, hills, castles and islands of Scotland.

Inside Westminster Abbey

22. The Stone of Destiny

If it is true that somewhere in Scotland the Stone of Destiny exists, then at some point it will turn up. It lies either deliberately hidden— underground or underwater, accidentally forgotten, or broken into pieces. How will it be identified?

Most experts today agree that the Stone described in early writings and shown on old seals, was considerably larger than the Westminster one, and there are so many references to 'marble', 'heiroglyphics' and 'hollows' that it was clearly made of some very hard stone, and decorated or inscribed in some way. We are also told it stood on legs.

The Stone of Destiny was a Christian symbol, rather than a pagan one. But crossing our fingers for luck to ward off the evil eye, and hanging pieces of our clothing on trees near certain wells shows late twentieth century Britons still performing pagan rituals— to be on the safe side. The Stone might have a Cross on it, and also spirals— for sun-worship. There could be Pictish symbols like the Boar, Irish emblems like the Harp, and so on. Then, as now, there was a to and fro of artistic ideas from one medium to another. Susan Youngs, Curator of Medieval and Later Antiquities at the British Museum, traces how the fine designs drawn by Irish and Scottish monastic illuminators inspired gold and silversmiths. Columba and Irish contemporaries produced beautifully illuminated gospels like the Book of Durrow and the Book of Kells— one of their inspirations was the fine metalwork of the day. The ancestor of a Lindisfarne animal scroll is found on a bowl at Sutton Hoo in Suffolk. Animal ornament probably came from Roman metal workers. Bede mentioned metalwork being brought in by Anglo-Saxon travellers, and through Dal Riada came Germanic designs and forms in the seventh century, on the evidence of Dunadd— a centre of fine metalwork, such as bird-headed brooches. Other finds at Craig Phadrig near Inverness show similar influences. Pictish stone-workers also found inspiration in these things, and we see the results scattered about Scotland from Sueno's Stone near Findhorn on the Moray Firth to the Latinus Stone at Whithorn, with a particularly rich collection in the triangle between Arbroath, Montrose and Meigle. With that amount of artistic precedent, and the stone-carving skills available at every stage of the Stone's story, there are few reasons to think it would be anything other than a most beautifully decorated artefact.

Norman Atkinson, Curator of Montrose Museum, is certain that the hollow on top is a footprint, because the custom of standing in the previous king's footprint was such a central feature of the early inauguration ceremonies. The Boar was a symbol of Pictish royalty— the one at Dunadd could not have been put there by a Dalriadic Scot, therefore it is more likely that it was the 'stamp' of Angus I, a Pict who must have been there by agreement because it was never removed or defaced.

Celtic peoples have always loved bright colours. There is the brilliant artistry of their illustrated manuscripts, and we can still see the painted carvings in some medieval churches. It is almost beyond doubt that such a revered object as the Stone of Destiny would not only have been elaborately carved, but also painted. The sort of colours and designs used by Edward I and Walter his Painter for their imitation Coronation Chair would certainly have been influenced by the original setting of the Stone at Scone.

Nigel Tranter has visualised the Stone in print. Thanks to his daring, we have a starting place for discussion. But both Norman Atkinson, and Rob Welsh of Angus Rock Art, believe the Stone would look rather different. They have committed their ideas to a model.

If the Stone of Destiny did originate in the Holy Land, as we saw in Chapter 5, it may well be composed of meteorite. If it came from Ireland or Iona, marble is the most likely material. Alternatively it may be basalt, black and polished with age. Least likely of all is sandstone, the material of the Stone Edward 1 took to Westminster.

Nigel Tranter believes
the Stone might look like this.

above and overleaf, left Some of the symbols one
might expect to see on an inaugural stone.

Robert of Gloucester said Scota 'broghte into Scotland a *whyte* marble ston'. The throne of Charlemagne was white marble— still visible at Aix-la-Chapelle in France.

The old seals appended to charters of the Scottish kings give us pictorial evidence. Made by highly skilled craftsmen, they were used over and over again on State documents. The makers would undoubtedly have been capable of producing good likenesses of the monarchs, just as coin-minters give us a recognisable Queen on our 50ps today. The seals were not photographs, so a certain amount of fashion, keeping up with the ruling Joneses of other nations, and omitting of less attractive features doubtless went on. Details of the King's accoutrements, his robes, and the seat on which he sat could have fallen into this category. Artistic licence permitted the inclusion of items that had some symbolic significance to the King and to Scotland. Kings' seals usually show the warrior King swashbuckling in his armour, riding a spirited horse and brandishing his sword, one one surface, while on the other he is seated with great dignity on the Stone of Destiny which is either bare, cushioned, or boxed.

Two seals are described as showing Edgar (1098-1107) 'sitting on a throne *or rather stool of*

right The Stone kept like a holy relic within a carved wooden seat with a richly embroidered cushion.

120

state; the legs terminating in eagle's claws' on charters in the Treasury of Durham Cathedral. There is another showing Alexander 1 'sitting on a chair of state . . . under each hand, on the field of the seal, is a roundle charged with some indistinct figure'. This seal seems to have been the model for the designs of several later versions, such as those of David 1 of Malcolm IV. The seal of William the Lion shows 'The King seated on a chair *or stool of state*'.

The seal of Alexander II (1214-1249) is of precisely the same design as that of William the Lion, but made in a more sophisticated style; the throne *or stool of state is more richly ornamented, and on each side is a branch of foliage*'. He is 'Seated on a throne, decorated with rich pannels and four finials of fleur-de-lis . . . his feet resting on two lizards'. Another of his shows enriched ornamentation on a throne *or stool of state.*

Balliol's seal is similar, showing him 'seated on a throne decorated with rich pannels and four crocketed pinnacles . . . on the dexter of throne is a shield, charged with an orle, the paternal arms of Balliol; on the sinister side is another, bearing a lion rampant'.

There is another, said to have been used after Balliol's Great Seal was broken up, for his authority was still recognised in Scotland. Here the King sits on a throne, the arms and legs of which are the heads and feet of animals.

There is even a seal showing Edward 1 of England, undated, and under the title of 'Deputy Governor of Scotland' he is seated on a throne, his feet resting on two lions.

If any of these seating arrangements include an accurate representation of the Stone of Destiny, and if it did indeed disappear in 1296, then

above Daniel in the lions' den depicted on the back of the Guinevere Stone at Meigle
left Pictish symbol

we should be able to discern some obvious change thereafter in the seals.

We have descriptions of the seals of Robert the Bruce (1306— 1329). One is appended to a Melrose Charter, dated 1317; 'The King, sitting on a throne, decorated in the same style as that of Balliol . . . his feet on two lizards'. Another dated 1320, shows Bruce 'seated on a throne or stool of state, the arms and legs of which are

Dr James Richardson noted that the spaces built to contain Edward I's Stone in the Westminster Chair *(left)* and the Stone of Destiny in Alexander's III's chair *(right)* at Scone were quite different.

formed of the legs of an animal and the bodies and heads of serpents, placed transversely, and over them is thrown embroiderd drapery'. Yet another shows him enthroned on 'a seat without back over which a draped cloth is thrown; the four corners of the seat are extended in the form of long curved necks and heads and legs of animals and the whole stands on a carved bracket.

In general, it has been taken that the word 'stool' means the Stone of Destiny. As far as is known the term 'stool' has not normally been used in descriptions of other medieval coronation ceremonies. The word 'throne' refers to a wooden structure in which the Stone was contained. This was most beautifully carved, with see-through sections in the manner in which holy relics were sometimes held, because that is how the Stone was regarded.

It is clear that a change of this sort took place. The early Kings sat quite comfortably on the Stone, with their knees forming a right-angle. Kings had to be of larger rather than smaller stature, as part of the physical image required of them, so these were relatively tall men. Even supposing they were only five feet eight inches, in order to sit like this the height of their seat would have to be 17inches (43 cm) high. In the later coronations the King has his feet well off the ground, and he is considerably diminished in proportion to his throne. The Westminster Stone is 11feet high.

The reference to the items on the sides of the seals are of interest. Alexander I has two round shield-like plaques. David I and Malcolm IV follow the same pattern. Alexander II has a 'branch of foliage' on either side. Balliol's seal has a shield on each side, one with his coat of arms, the other carrying the lion rampant. There may be some connection between this recurring pair of plaques and public identification, through knowledge of heraldry, of the office of the personage on the seal and/or the realm he represents.

The second feature of interest is the use of animal imagery. Edgar's 'stool' has legs terminating in eagle's claws, Alexander III rests his own feet on two lizards and his 'stool' is ornamented with two lions' heads in cusped panels. The second Balliol seal shows the king on his throne 'the arms and legs of which are formed of the heads and feet of animals'. Even Edward 1, acting 'Deputy Governor' rests his feet on two lions. With Bruce we have the description of a throne 'decorated in the same style as that of Balliol, the arms and legs of which are formed of the legs of an animal, and the bodies and heads of serpents. We also have the reappearance of the lizards last seen some fifty years earlier, well before the visit of Edward 1.

As the old Stone of Destiny moved through Scottish history it probably collected decoration appropriate to each era. The 'Guinever Stone' is perhaps the best example of such a re-cycled monument, and suggest the type of decoration we might expect to find. First carved with cup-and-ring symbols between 2,000 and 500 BC, from the 8th to 10th centuries AD a 'ring of glory' filled with a cross was carved at the top, embellished with raised bosses thought to have been inspired by the rivet heads used in the art of metal-working jewellery-makers. The rest of this face is taken up with animals, serpents and the figures of people, now believed to carry some of the Arthurian story. The other side contains an iconography very popular in medieval central Scotland, that of Daniel in the Lion's Den. The stone was found this century, in use as a graveslab. In May 1991, after a life spent studying early manuscripts, Professor Norma Goodrich, a Californian historian, positively identified the Guinevere Stone as a reworked section from the triptych funeral-stone of King Arthur's Queen, who is believed to have died nearby in the sixth century. Now it has pride of place in Meigle Museum, near Coupar Angus, as a focus for tourists, art lovers and historians.

So the Stone we are looking for stands at least 17 inches high, 18 inches deep and 32 inches wide. It is dark, polished and painted, with some spirals, a hollow in the top not unlike a footprint. There will be traces of carved lettering probably in Latin, possibly in Gaelic, once picked out in red and white or into which precious metal has been run. There may be several other carvings,

such as the Irish Harp, a Pictish Boar, Daniel and his lions. It has legs or feet like eagle's claws and, running up and down the front edges, the legs of animals, possibly lizards. On either side pairs of crook-shaped hooks were fixed so that it could be slung on two poles for transport.

We have already noted how Walter Scott's love for Melrose Abbey was translated into his

A stool with animal legs, feet and arms.

removal of some of the ancient stones for the building of Abbotsford. The Stone that may have marked the grave of King Arthur, not far from that of his Queen, was blown up for use as building material for Arthurstone House, not far from Meigle. In Forteviot the carved faces of stone can be seen on the outside walls of some of the houses— who knows what may lie hidden within? Chunks of the Council Table at Finlaggan may be hidden in drystane dykes or built into the foundations of Islay farmhouses. It is worth keeping an eye open wherever you travel in Scotland.

23. Freedom Come-All-Ye

Having scrutinised the ancient writings, looked at the legends, mulled over the myths and considered several histories of Scotland, where does that leave the story of the Stone of Destiny today, and what does it matter as we approach the millenium? Perhaps the writings of poets, novelists, politicians and ordinary people are what matters now, and they have all had their say, at one time or another, about the Stone, and how it symbolises the relationship between Scotland and England. Perhaps they should be allowed the last word.

Robert Louis Stevenson (1850-94) wrote of that relationship: 'Here are two people almost identical in blood, language and religion, and yet a few years of quarrelsome isolation . . . have so separated their thoughts and ways, that not unions, nor mutual dangers, nor steamers nor railways, nor all the Kings' horses and all the King's men seem able to obliterate the broad distinction'.

The lives of many people have been affected by the efforts they have made to have the Westminster Stone returned to Scotland. Of what relevance are all these stones— who cares whether or not the Stone of Destiny still exists, and that a non-representative group of people may be holding an object of national interest? From the constant stream of correspondence to newspapers, quite a number of people care.

When, in 1951, John Rollo had the Westminster Stone, he decided he'd better find out exactly where he stood. He engaged a legal friend in casual discussion; 'Suppose someone received the Stone of Destiny and looked after it, knowing nothing about its taking, was given it in Scotland and simply acted as a caretaker. If he was found in possession of it what would the charge be?' Quoth the lawyer, 'If he knew nothing of it, he was no party to the English charge of Sacrilege. If it could be proved that it was stolen property, and it was given to him in Scotland, then he was a re-setter in Scots law. But before a charge of re-set could be raised, ownership of the alleged Stone articles would have to be proved, and this would be the crux of the whole thing.' Rollo laughed. What right had the English Crown to possession?

Arnold Kemp, editor of the *Herald*, when asked for his current thoughts about the the Stone, says:

> It depends on whether you approach the question from a point of strict legality. Scotland's constitutional arrangments are governed by the Treaty of Union and its sovereignty is vested in the Union. In turn UK sovereignty is said to reside in the monarch in Parliament. London, on these grounds, can claim the Stone, which is of course the symbol of Scottish sovereignty.

Hamish Henderson sings of freedom, in Strichen, Aberdeenshire

'This, however, is carrying matters too far. The decision not to return the Stone to Scotland was probably partly motivated by a desire not to encourage what was seen as an act of theft. But it was also one of the several crass decisions that were taken around the time—eg the Queen received the Honours of Scotland in mufti, a decision was taken to call her Queen Elizabeth II, and so on. Whatever the legality, the Stone belongs to Scotland spiritually and morally, and should be returned there. The contemporary spirit of Scotland, I am sure, is that sovereignty resides with the people (as, indeed, it does in most democratic constitutions). On these grounds, therefore, the Stone should be returned.

'The Stone, like other symbols of state, indeed has significance because it gives material expression to the abstract concept of Scottish sovereignty and proof of the claim that Scotland remains a nation, though in Union with England. I am strongly of the view that the Stone should be returned to Scotland. From this you may guess that I support Home Rule!'

Kay Matheson campaigned actively for the same ideal, but eventually buried her energies in the Gaeltachd. She is still fiercely proud of the part she played in taking the Stone. From the Nursing Home where she now lives, across the loch from the village in which she spent most of her adult life, she looks back at the events of 1950. 'It was important, because it brought attention to the neglect of Scotland. The further north you went away from London, from the centre of Government, the dearer things became—yet it was supposed to be a United Kingdom. And if it's united then everything should be equal'.

She has no regrets although 'it has affected my life—very much so. Taking the Stone served the purpose. What we did wakened the Scots people up a bit. The Scottish people are less apathetic now. A lot of the English who come up here have come to see me about it.' She worries that 'the English are trying to take over in a different way now. That's what puts a lot of people off the Sassenachs. They come to a place and they think "peasants up here—we'll just show them" and it's in their sheer ignorance, in their innocent inexperience. They genuinely believe that they are better than us.'

Ian Hamilton, having published his books about the 1951 Stone-taking, knows better than anyone that the idea 'has never died.

For a long while it was to my annoyance that I was referred to as "The Stone of Destiny Man"—but I could be labelled with a lot worse things . . . After all to try and stir up your country to re mind it that it has got a soul is a laudable ambition for any young man, and I am intensely proud that it was I who had that ambition. There's a lot to be said for the Stone being in Westminster because the Scottish people, insofar as they think of it, they think "oh that's in Westminster and it shouldn't be", whereas if it was with the rest of the Scottish Regalia in Edinburgh Castle no-one would pay any attention to it, because only American tourists go to see it.

'Without any doubt the Scots are better than they were nearly forty years ago . . . Now, one could say, there is definitely a Scottish nation and a Scottish national culture. Glasgow's Mayfest is a perfect example of that. Glasgow's an exciting place to be. In my profession the anglicised accent is only adopted by the minority of advocates—most advocates now prefer to speak the way their parents spoke, and I think that's a very real improvement. The people I appear with and for in court and the juries I address daily can never be anything other than Scottish even although since 1707 they haven't had a government. A nation that can survive without a government is a very real nation indeed. It's in our language, and in the way we approach problems—and of course I'm very conscious of it in the law. If people are daft enough to vote for one or other of the parties who want us to be governed four hundred miles away from the south east corner of the island they deserve all they get. I keep asking myself if I'm a political Home Rule man and the answer always comes out "yes I am." It may well be that Edward I was tricked. The remarkable

a friend, Kenny MacKenzie, set up Castle Wynd printers in Edinburgh in the fifties and published four volumes of Hugh MacDiarmid's poetry, including *A Drunk Man Looks at the Thistle*. He says now it was 'the proudest thing I have done with my life.' He wrote a prize-winning play about 'the Scots and their inability to cope with disaster in any other way than by singing romantic songs.' Now a QC, he says; 'I'll die a pauper

Ian Hamilton *left* holds the sixth-century Bachall of Lismore. 'A nation that can survive without a government is a very real nation indeed.' Nigel Tranter *right* keeps his crumb of the Stone beneath the seat of a tiny silver coronation chair.

thing is that if he was duped no-one ever came forward with the real Stone, although the country was pretty well fought over for eighteen years.

Hamilton's life zig-zagged, after 1951, between the legal profession and many others. He helped

because I've always had something more interesting to do than put money away for my old age. I don't intend to have an old age anyway.' It is unlikely that Hamilton knows more than he is saying about the Westminster Stone's provenance. I received a letter from Ayrshire, telling of a dark stone with a ring visible, which is built into the side of the Fairlieburn near Mary Queen of Scots bridge, reminding me 'Ian Hamilton used to live in Fairlie' and a new rumour is born.

Both Gavin Vernon and Alan Stuart ducked out of the limelight. Vernon made for the far side of Canada, while Stuart remained in the West of Scotland, claiming that he was no longer 'a political animal'. His brother Ronald thinks the

Other old stalwarts, such as Wendy Wood, Bertie Gray, John MacCormack and John Rollo, are long dead.

Everyone involved in the 1950 taking of the Stone was given a crumb, and each keeps it in a different way. Ronald Stuart had his set in a kiltpin, Nigel Tranter has his beneath the seat of a tiny silver coronation chair. He subscribes to the theory that the Westminster Stone originated

Naomi Mitchison *left* says she could have hidden the Stone amongst other stones in the Carradale river. Arnold Kemp *right*—'The Stone belongs to Scotland spiritually and morally, and should be returned.'

business of the Westminster Stone 'was an opportunity missed'. If the authorities had acceded to the Scottish request to hold coronations in Scotland, or had allowed the Stone to stay in Scotland, they would have won over so many people.

in Perthshire, and includes his theories of what happened to the old Stone in several novels. His friend Joan Earle suggests the stone at present beneath the Coronation Chair may be a replica—perhaps even fibreglass—pointing out that it would be common sense on the part of the authorities to hide away the 'real' thing.

Eleven inches is the height of a decent-sized Victorian chamber pot. Any monarch sitting on a stone of such meagre dimensions would have looked utterly ridiculous—even the knees of a relatively small man would have been up around his ears. Try it. Would you crown a king, who was supposed to look heroic and dignified, on such a thing?

I carried out a small survey among students, teenagers, and women living in an area of urban deprivation, who could have been forgiven for ignoring anything but the problems of their own lives, to find out if anyone nowadays had heard of the Stone of Destiny. Most had, saying that it had been taken from Westminster at some time. Some had tales to tell about it that diverged a little from actuality, embroidering it here, darning the hole made by a forgotten detail with threads of imagination there, again demonstrating how folk-tale begins. They were unanimous in saying that the Stone should be kept in Scotland.

Some other people were invited to give their views on the Stone. John Smith MP and leader of the Labour Party says 'I do not think too much significance should be attached either to the Stone of Destiny or where it is located,' and it appears that MPs Paddy Ashdown, Ian Lang and Malcolm Rifkind agree with him. In spite of the fact that the Prince of Wales happily pronounces on topics ranging from architecture to other people's cars, and may one day have to sit athwart whatever stone lies in Westminster he, like the Queen, 'makes it a rule not to comment'. Jim Sillars of the SNP writes more openly, 'I don't think there is any doubt that the Stone of Destiny should be located in Scotland because of its symbolic link with our past. Donald Dewar MP is thoughtful; 'The Stone is associated in most people's minds with Kingship and coronations, and whatever the views about the political shape of the United Kingdom few people seem to favour breaking the traditional links with the Crown. For myself, the Stone is a symbol of the continuity of Scotland's history and a reminder of our stormy relationship with our neighbours in medieval times. There is a case for its return to Scotland . . . A good deal of thought would have to be given to the right setting for it, and I would not want to invest it with a political significance which I think is somewhat forced. I am interested in finding practical solutions to the problem of Government and making a partnership work.'

Recalling the events of 1951, Naomi Mitchison writes; 'At the time, I could have hidden the Stone by putting it into Carradale river at a place where it would be among other stones . . . It was a good game of hide and seek while it lasted.' She thinks that 'what is supposed today to be the particular stone, may not be', but if it *is*, then perhaps it should be kept wherever Scottish affairs are being dealt with—'it might have to be carried round by the Scottish representative in Europe.'

A note arrives, from an address in Bexhill-on-Sea, including yet another version of the legend, as it was told the writer fifty years ago when she was a child in Ireland. 'A king of Scotland demanded it of the High King of Ireland. The latter being a wily man and not wishful to quarrel with his neighbour, who was probably stronger than him, cut a piece of black stone, had a mason carve a few runes on it, and sent it to Scotland. The true stone of Destiny remains on the Hill of Tara to this day!'

Florence M. Russell of Greenock enthuses, 'Can you imagine what the discovery of the real one would do for this half-dead country?'
Maybe the Knights Templar and the Revd Mackay Nimmo guard the true Stone of Destiny. But when the stone they delivered to the People's Palace in 1990 was examined, its very convincing crack was found to have been chiselled

superficially on only two surfaces —it did not go through the stone at all, proving that it had never been broken. Neither trace of bronze dowels nor of any other metal was found, proving conclusively that this stone is not the one which Bertie Gray mended. Ian Hamilton corroborated this when he declared that it was certainly not the Stone he brought home from Westminster.

Looking back over the countless legends about the Stone, which seem determined to survive, it is tempting to ask—what use is it to the people of Scotland to rake over the dead coals, the dying fires of national fervour, at a time when the whole of Britain is likely to be melted down in the furnace of European unification? Of what possible relevance could the folklore of the worn-out apathetic dregs of a people, living on the fringes of northern Europe, be to the world at large?

Rosalind Mitchison, Professor Emeritus of Social History at the University of Edinburgh, daughter-in-law of Naomi Mitchison, and a non-Scot, said in a talk at the 1991 Edinburgh Book Festival: 'Well, you don't want to lose a species from the world. The Scots were one of the earliest peoples of the world to express a feeling of nationality'.

If nothing else Scotland and her traditions are a curiosity. Will her destiny join that of her Stone—will she too disappear in a miasma of soap-opera and sentiment, to walk off hand in hand into the sunset with England?

Medieval historian Alexander Grant of Lancaster University said of the Scottish perspective, 'It's good for debunking English history in the eyes of the world'. He points out that the Scots, being one of the family of West European peoples, 'played their part in, and so have their contribution to make to, the wider field of European history'. So hard have Scottish historians had to work at discovering the roots of their civilisation, and so honestly and painstakingly

have they done this, that they are now in demand to write the histories of other countries. Scots have proved themselves to be exceptional the world over, and in many countries over the centuries have become key people. Nowadays, with a few drunken exceptions, Scots are welcome everywhere for their intelligence, their straightforwardness and their wit. Singer-broadcaster Jimmie MacGregor notes that despite the fearsome economic and social problems of Scotland, 'humour will continue to be a potent weapon.'

Nobody would advocate pointless bloody revolution on such a hard working, laughter loving, peaceful crowd, but a modicum of self-determination is surely not too much to ask. This is necessary if Scots are to take an interest in their own affairs, if apathy is to be kept at bay. As things are, we do not insist on the teaching of our own history in our schools, though a little is permitted if there is a teacher who happens to have the appropriate knowledge. Instead, we allow our understanding of ourselves to be peddled to us by the saleable nostalgia of the tourist industry, and moulded by the meagre requirements of the Scottish Examination Board.

So why do we not simply merge with England and stop going on about 'the Scottish people'? For there is no such thing as Scottish blood. On the contrary, the people of Scotland are a polyglot collection of immigrants who have been arriving since the last ice-age. So are the people of England. As we have seen in the present century, it takes only a few generations for races to mix and blend. Why is it, then, that in spite of this, and of all the efforts made over the centuries to unite these two nations through force, political union, joint monarchs, there is still such a feeling of separateness in Scotland? And if they feel so disadvantaged, what is it that time and time again stops them from devolving a Scottish Parliament to themselves?

Now, when the world is fragmenting into bite-sized units within larger contexts, when peoples are showing a desire to take the running of their own affairs off the shoulders of large conglomerate empires,whether communist or not, and when nations with far greater difficulties than Scotland are creaking into action, why do Scots not simply follow the fashion? Much smaller units within Britain—Jersey, the Isle of Man—have been self-governing for years.

Of the many nations currently exploding into racial hatred across the world, most operate through bigotry, bitterness and bloodshed. It should be easier here, in a democracy, to make changes peacefully, given sensitivity and understanding on both sides, given the will to effect improvement. Perhaps those in power at Westminster will have taken heed of the fact that revolutions are not started by crowds of ordinary people, who simply want to get on with their ordinary lives, but by relatively small acts on the part of individuals, artists, writers, idealistic students. A vegetable seller called Jenny Geddes threw a stool at Dean Hannay in St Giles Cathedral on 23 July 1637 and started a rebellion that ended with the decapitation of Charles 1. What did a QC and a teacher start when, at Christmas 1950, they took a Stone from Westminster?

The legends and facts presented in these pages will, it is hoped, have made for interesting reading, but do they amount to anything more than romantic tales? The answer to that may be nearer than at any time in the past 285 years. Scotland is a small country. Its population of five million is draining away southward, set to dwindle by eleven percent in the next twenty years. In 1992 the Scottish people are only in direct control of eleven percent of the revenue they raise. Yet sometimes it seems their sense of national identity is satisfied by singing maudlin songs in pubs, enthusing over football teams, and moaning vaguely, inactively, about English control. Over one third of them don't even feel it's worth the effort to go out and vote when they do get the chance.

The Scottish Convention is a powerless but well-intentioned body of individuals representing many interests who have thought it worthwhile to spend time deliberating, sometimes intelligently, sometimes with passion, on how a devolved assembly could be organised, and how realised. It deserves the serious attention of the Scottish people, their elected representatives of all parties, and of the Westminster Parliament. It deserves action.

To be conscious of our nationality is not to be exclusive. We all declare multiple allegiances. The fact that we enjoy being Scottish or Welsh or Pakistani does not exclude the possibility of our being something else too. We feel proud of being, say, an Aberdonian, and that as such we are different from—and very possibly superior to—a Glaswegian. People are more inclined to be boastful about being a Highlander than a Lowlander, about being 'working class' than 'middle class'—yet on occasion most of us also describe our nationality as British. To the rest of the world we are just Europeans. The more we become a tiny European state, the more we will need to feel firmly rooted in our own topography, history and genealogy, with all its folklore and traditions.

Whether or not the Stone of Scone was ever the Stone of Destiny, it remains a symbol of great potency to both Scots and English. As we have seen, the English hang onto it with every security device, every legal circomlocution known to man. If it goes missing they move heaven and earth to get it back. It does not belong to them. The Stone cannot in itself solve Scotland's problems. But its return—or the return of its current representative—would be a gesture which would go some way to removing harmful resentment between north and south, would suggest the beginning of what could be a new and fruitful mutual respect. Such a gesture of popular goodwill would harm nobody. Crowds would still fill the collecting boxes at Westminster Abbey. The English people and their Westminster Dean and Chapter and their Royal Peculiar should now honour their seven hundred year-old treaty by returning a Stone which remains a lasting symbol of their duplicity. The story of the Stone of Destiny is a broken thread in the rich fabric of Scotland's oral history. In order to complete the pattern, the Stone in Westminster, whether or not it is the 'real' one, should be returned. It's the thought that counts.

We are in a new situation, in the nineties, where with consideration on both sides we may be able to demonstrate a more comfortable way of declaring our allegiances, our roots, our race, where we come from, than through war, and thus build up mutual trust and honest relationships with all our neighbours.

It is fortunate for the UK as a whole that Scots are no longer inclined to resort to violence. This should now be met with an imaginative, generous and forward-looking response in which the Crown and the vast weight of English parliamentarians should rise to the peaceful challenge of Scotland, should listen to the voice of its people, its Convention, and its wish to have its Stone back. They should return it. Now.

For how long must the Stone keep its secret and its guardians shroud it in mystery?

131

THE FREEDOM COME-ALL-YE

Roch the wind in the clear day's dawnin',
  Blaws the cloods heelster gowdy ow'r the bay.
But there's mair nor a cauld wind blawin'
  Through the great glen o' the warld the day.
It's a thocht that will gar oor rottans -
  a' they rogues that gan gallus fresh and gay -
Tak' the road an' seek ither loanins
  For their ill ploys tae sport an' play.

Nae mair will the bonnie callants
  Mairch tae war, when oor braggarts crousely craw,
Nor wee weans frae pit-heid an' clachan
  Mourn the ships sailin' doon the Broomielaw.
Broken faimlies in lands we've herriet
  Will curse Scotland the Brave nae mair, nae mair;
Black an' white, ane til ither mairriet
  Mak' the vile barracks o' their maisters bare.

O come all ye at hame wi' freedom,
  Never heed whit the hoodies croak for doom;
In your hoose a' the bairns o' Adam
  Can find breid, barley bree an' painted room.
When Maclean meets wi's freens in Springburn
  A' the roses an' geans will turn tae bloom,
And a black boy frae yont Nyanga
  Dings the fell gallows o' the burghers doon.

Hamish Henderson

REFERENCE SOURCES AND BIBLIOGRAPHY

1. *Carried Away At Christmas*
A SENSE OF TREASON, Ian Hamilton. Lochar, 1990
THE TAKING OF THE STONE OF DESTINY, Ian Hamilton
Q.C. Lochar, 1991
GLASGOW HERALD, SCOTSMAN

2. *The Hostage Stone*
A SENSE OF TREASON, Ian Hamilton Q.C. Lochar, 1990
YOURS SINCERELY FOR SCOTLAND, Wendy Wood. Barker
1970
B.B.C. RECORDING OF JOHN ROLLO
GLASGOW HERALD, SCOTSMAN, ARBROATH HERALD

3. *Kings, Queens and Coronation Chairs*
WESTMINSTER ABBEY OFFICIAL GUIDE, Dean & Chapter
of Westminster, 1988
THE CORONATION STONE, Professor William Skene.
Edmonston & Douglas, Edinburgh, 1869
YOURS SINCERELY FOR SCOTLAND, Wendy Wood, Barker,
1970

4. *How the Legends Began*
ALBION, Jennifer Westwood. Collins, 1985
ARGYLL THE ENDURING HEARTLAND, Marion Campbell.
Turnstone Books, London,1977
FIRESIDE TALES OF THE TRAVELLER CHILDREN, Duncan
Williamson. Canongate, 1983
LOCHFYNESIDE, Alexander Fraser. St Andrew Press, 1971
PROCEEDINGS OF THE SOCIETY OF ANTIQUARIES OF
SCOTLAND
THE CORONATION STONE, William Skene. Edinburgh, 1869
SCOTS MAGAZINE Article by Archie McKerracher Dec 1984,
Aug 1989

5. *Jacob and the Thunderstones*
KING JAMES VI TRANSLATION OF THE OLD TESTAMENT
WESTERN CIVILIZATION, Diane W. Darst. McGraw-Hill,1990
THE HOLY CITIES OF ARABIA,Eldon Rutter. New York,1928

6. *Ireland*
CELTIC MYTHOLOGY, Ward Rutherford. Aquarian
Press,1987
PRE-CHRISTIAN IRELAND,Peter Harbison. Thames &
Hudson, 1988
LEBOR GABALA ERENN, ed R.A.S. Macalister. 1920's Irish
Texts Society vols 34, 35, 39, 41,& 44
TIMES ATLAS OF WORLD HISTORY, 1989 EDITION, Guild

AN IONA ANTHOLOGY, ed. F. Marian McNeill. New Iona
Press

7. *Romans and Christians*
HISTORY OF SCOTLAND,Peter & Fiona Somerset Fry.
Routledge, 1985
SCOTS MAGAZINE Article by Janet B. Christie, Nov. 1970
A CELTIC SAGA, Andrew R.M.Patterson. St Andrew Press,
1991
THE WHITHORN DIG, Peter Hill & Dave Pollock. Whithorn
Trust 1991
WHITHORN 3, EXCAVATIONS, Peter Hill, 1990
GUIDEBOOK TO MELROSE ABBEY, 1888
MELROSE ABBEY, H.M.S.O., 1990
EXPLORING SCOTLAND'S HERITAGE, DUMFRIES &
GALLOWAY, Geoffrey Stell. Royal Commission on the
Ancient and Historical Monuments of Scotland 1986
SCOTLAND, THE MAKING OF A KINGDOM, A.A.M.
Duncan, Oliver & Boyd 1978

8. *Dalriada and the Royal Boar*
EXPLORING SCOTLAND'S HERITAGE - ARGYLL & THE
WESTERN ISLES, Graham Ritchie & Mary Harman. Royal
Commission on Ancient & Historical Monuments of Scotland,
1985
THE PREHISTORIC ROCK ART OF ARGYLL, Ronald W. B.
Morris. Dolphin, 1977
SCOTLAND, THE MAKING OF A KINGDOM, A.A.M.
Duncan. Oliver & Boyd, 1978

9. *Columba King of Storms*
IONA, Dr Mairi MacArthur. E.U.P., 1990
LIFE OF COLUMBA, ed Wm Reeves, 1844
COLUMBA, Ian Finlay. Richard Drew, 1990
THE CRUTHIN, Ian Adamson. Pretani, 1986
ISLANDS, P. A. MacNab. David & Charles,1987
IONA, Fiona Macleod. Floris, 1982
AN IONA ANTHOLOGY, ed F. Marian McNeill. New Iona
Press, 1991
PROCEEDINGS OF SOC OF ANTIQUARIES OF SCOTLAND
Vol 12 1854

10. *Dunstaffnage*
EXPLORING SCOTLAND'S HERITAGE - ARGYLL & THE
WESTERN ISLES, Graham Ritchie & Mary Harman. Royal
Commission on Ancient & Historical Monuments of Scotland,
1985

DUNSTAFFNAGE CASTLE AND THE STONE OF DESTINY,
Dr W. Douglas Simpson. Edinburgh, 1958
KENNETH, Nigel Tranter. Hodder, 1990
SCOTS MAGAZINE, Article by Lorn MacIntyre June '90

11. *Scotland United?*
SCOTLAND, THE MAKING OF A KINGDOM, A.A.M.Duncan.
Oliver & Boyd, 1978.
SCOTLAND FROM THE EARLIEST TIMES, Croft Dickinson,
revised A.A.M. Duncan
HISTORY OF SCOTLAND, Somerset Frys. Routledge, 1985
SCOTLAND, A NEW HISTORY, Michael Lynch. Century 1991
THE STORY OF SCOTLAND Sunday Mail
KENNETH, Nigel Tranter. Hodder, 1990

12. *Who Owns Scotland?*
SCOTLAND UNDER HER EARLIEST KINGS VOL III, E. W.
Robertson, 1862
ALEXANDER III, James Ferguson. Maclehose, 1937
THE HISTORY OF ENGLAND, Jasper Ridley. Routledge, 1981
HISTORY OF SCOTLAND, Somerset Fry. Routledge, 1985
YOURS SINCERELY FOR SCOTLAND, Wendy Wood. Barker,
1970
MONARCHS OF SCOTLAND, Stewart Ross. Lochar, 1990

13. *England's Edward and the Celtic Fringes*
THE MIDDLE AGES, R. J. Cootes. Longman, 1972
PELICAN HISTORY VOL 3, Doris Mary Stenton.Penguin 1972
MEDIEVAL & TUDOR BRITAIN, Valerie E. Chancellor.
Penguin, 1978
THE STORY OF SCOTLAND, Nigel Tranter. Routledge, 1987
THE HISTORY OF ENGLAND, Jasper Ridley. Routledge,1981
BRUCE TRILOGY, Nigel Tranter. Hodder, 1971-72
SCOTTISH HISTORICAL REVIEW (Vol xxxviii) Article by
Dominica Legge, p109 - 113
SCOTS MAGAZINE, November 1970
PROCEEDINGS OF THE SOCIETY OF ANTIQUARIES OF
LONDON

14. *Wallace and the Missing Stone*
SCOTTISH CHIEFS, Jane Porter. 1810
CELTIC SCOTLAND, W. Skene. 1876 - 80
THE WALLACE, Nigel Tranter. Hodder, 1975
SCOTLAND, THE MAKING OF A KINGDOM, A.A.M.Duncan.
Oliver & Boyd, 1978
SCOTLAND, A NEW HISTORY, Michael Lynch. Century, 1991

15. *Robert the Bruce*
THE BRUCE, John Barbour, ed A.A.H. Douglas. McClellan,
1964
ROBERT THE BRUCE AND THE SCOTTISH IDENTITY,
Geoffrey Barrow. Saltire, 1984

THE HISTORY OF ENGLAND
        Jasper Ridley. Routledge 1981
ROBERT THE BRUCE, Ronald McNair Scott. Canongate, 1982
ROBERT THE BRUCE, Alan Bold. Pitkin
THE BRUCE TRILOGY, Nigel Tranter. Hodder, 1971-72
STORY OF SCOTLAND, Sunday Mail, 1988

16. *Lord of the Isles*
ISLAY, Norman Newton. David & Charles, 1988
THE LORDS OF THE ISLES, Ronald Williams. Chatto, 1984
THE LANDS OF THE LORDSHIP, Domhnall MacEacharna
Argyll,1976
JAMES IV, Norman MacDougall. John Donald, 1989
FINLAGGAN INTERIM REPORT & UPDATE, David Caldwell.
National Museums of Scotland, 1991

17.   *The Search for the Stone of Skye*
THE LANDS OF THE LORDSHIP, Domhnall MacEacharna.
Argyll 1976
THE MEDIEVAL CASTLES OF SKYE & LOCHALSH, Roger
Miket & David L. Roberts. MacLean, 1990
CEANNAS NAN GAIDHEAL Clan Donald Lands Trust, 1985

18. *The Knights Templar*
KNIGHTS OF ST JOHN OF JERUSALEM IN SCOTLAND, ed
Dr Ian B. Cowan, Dr P.H.R. Mackay & Dr ALan Macquarrie.
Scottish History Society, Edinburgh, 1983
SCOTS MAGAZINE, June 1991 p261, Article by Archie
        McKerracher

19. *Sir Walter Scott and Edinburgh Castle*
SCOTTISH CHIEFS, Miss Jane Porter. Routledge, 1857
TALES OF A GRANDFATHER, Sir Walter Scott
A JOURNEY TO THE WESTERN ISLANDS OF SCOTLAND,
Johnson & Boswell, ed R.W. Chapman. O.U.P. 1970
EDINBURGH CASTLE, Official Guide Books
H.M.S.O. 1966 and 1989
GUIDE TO ABBOTSFORD, Abbotsford
PROCEEDINGS OF THE SOCIETY OF ANTIQUARIES OF
SCOTLAND vols 4 & 100

20. *Macbeth's Castle*
HIGHWAYS AND BYWAYS IN THE CENTRAL HIGHLANDS,
Seton Gordon. MacMillan, 1948
RAMBLES IN FORFARSHIRE, James Myles. Dundee, 1850
PICTURES OF SCOTLAND, Robert Chambers. 1828
OLD STORIES IN STONE, Alexander Hutcheson. Kidd,
Dundee, 1927
THE EARLY CHRONICLES RELATING TO SCOTLAND, Sir
H.E. Maxwell. Maclehose, 1912
THE STORY OF SCOTLAND IN STONE, Ian C. Hannah.
Oliver & Boyd 1934

STONES OF DESTINY, George Ritchie, Kirk Session, Scone, 1986
STATISTICAL ACCOUNTS OF SCOTLAND 1798 and 1857
SCOTS MAGAZINE May 1954, Nov. 1975, Dec. 1984, Aug. 1989
MINUTES OF THE SOCIETY OF ANTIQUARIES OF LONDON Vol XXXIV 1817 - 1823
PROCEEDINGS OF THE SOCIETY OF ANTIQUARIES OF SCOTLAND 1857 Vol II, 8th March 1869
THE TIMES 1st Jan. 1819
LONDON MORNING CHRONICLE Jan. - Feb. 1819
EDINBURGH EVENING CHRONICLE Jan. - Feb. 1819
CALEDONIAN MERCURY 7th Jan. 1819.
INVERNESS COURIER 27th Feb. 1951
PAPER ON SCONE AND THE STONE OF DESTINY, Lady Pamela Mansefield

21. A Royal Peculiar
DAILY TELEGRAPH: Daily Telegraph 23rd Oct. 1974

22. The Stone of Destiny
COLUMBA, Ian Finlay. Richard Drew, 1990
EARLY CELTIC ART, Ruth and Vincent Megaw. Shire, 1986
THE WORK OF ANGELS, ed Sue Youngs. British Museum, 1989
THE BOOK OF KELLS Thames & Hudson, 1980
DARK AGE SCULPTURE National Museums of Antiquities of Scotland
PICTS, Anna Ritchie. Historic Buildings & Monuments, 1989
NIGEL TRANTER'S SCOTLAND Richard Drew, 1981

DESCRIPTIVE CATALOGUE OF THE GREAT SEALS AND SIGNETS OF THE KINGS OF SCOTLAND
STORY OF SCOTLAND IN STONE, Ian C. Hannah. Oliver & Boyd 1934

23. Freedom Come-All-Ye
A SCHEME OF HOME RULE WITH REFERENCE TO SCOTLAND, Eric Macdonald Lockhart, Counsellor at Law. Berry, Glasgow, 1886

General
CAMBRIDGE HISTORICAL ENCYCLOPEDIA OF GREAT BRITAIN AND IRELAND, ed Christopher Haig. C.U.P. 1990
ECOLOGICAL IMPERIALISM THE BIOLOGICAL EXPANSION OF EUROPE 900 - 1900, Alfred W. Crosby. C.U.P. 1986
TIMES ATLAS OF WORLD HISTORY 3RD EDITION, ed. Norman Stone. Guild, 1989
THE NATURE OF SCOTLAND, ed. Magnus Magnusson. Canongate, 1991
TOURING MAP OF SCOTLAND, Geographica, Edinburgh
ORDNANCE SURVEY PATHFINDER SERIES OF MAPS, Ordnance Survey, Southampton
ORDNANCE SURVEY LANDRANGER SERIES, Ordnance Survey, Southampton
VARIOUS GUIDEBOOKS TO CASTLES, H.M.S.O.
A GUIDE TO THE ABBEYS OF SCOTLAND, Anthony New, Constable, London 1988